Luke Wroblewski

MOBILE FIRST

D0591370

Publisher: Jeffrey Zeldman
Designer: Jason Santa Maria
Editor: Mandy Brown
Copyeditor: Krista Stevens
Compositor: Rob Weychert

ISBN 978-1-937557-02-7

A Book Apart
New York, New York
http://abookapart.com

10 9 8 7 6 5 4 3 2 1

TABLE OF CONTENTS

FOREWORD

Luke Wroblewski is a data guy, so let's check the stats. He has personally written 1,372 articles, given 190 presentations, and authored three books on mobile and web usability, interaction, and design, his latest and (I think) most important being the one you now hold in your hands. If that kind of output leaves you unimpressed, consider that Luke did all this writing in his free time, while employed as digital product design lead for some of the biggest companies on the internet and occasionally at his own startups.

This highly accomplished, green-shirted, plain-spoken designer has spent the past several years focusing intensely on the mobile experience. That is lucky for him, as mobile is where the whole web and world are going in a headlong rush. It's even luckier for you and me, because Luke not only knows mobile inside-out and backwards, he's also a brilliant designer who puts the user first. Plus he's a heck of a great communicator. Luke writes from a foundation of 16 years of thought leadership and digital product design execution—not to mention the absorption of thousands of white papers, internal reports, articles, books, and lectures. And he has poured what he knows into every page of *Mobile First*.

Reading this book is not only fun, it's painlessly but profoundly educational. Luke's call to action is changing the way my company and I approach the design of websites, and it will change the way you do, too. *Mobile First* is packed with the best kind of persuasion—persuasion from data, letting the facts shriek for themselves. And it offers the best kind of advice: practical, immediate, user-focused, big-picture stuff that sweats every detail and respects your IQ and your experience as a practitioner.

I love this book. I'm thrilled that we were lucky enough to publish it. I hope it ends up on every designer, front-end developer, and UX person's bookshelf. I want to see our industry embrace the mobile experience in a way that helps our users and us not merely succeed online but thrive. If enough of us follow the precepts of this little book, I am confident about the future of the web.

—Jeffrey Zeldman

INTRODUCTION

THIS BOOK IS REALLY just a small, simple idea. But like many other simple ideas before it, this idea has deep and far-reaching implications. It changes how we define the personal computer and how we use the web. While that's a very big deal, it can be boiled down to how we get started.

Mobile first

For years, most web teams have designed products and information for desktop and laptop computers. For these teams, mobile was an afterthought if even a thought at all. Sadly, this approach actually made sense in many parts of the world for quite a while. Browsing the web on mobile phones was painful; carriers controlled access to the web on their devices; and mobile network speeds often made everything grind to a halt. Very few people used the web on mobiles (unless they were in Japan), and those that did were usually faced with an unpleasant experience.

But things have changed so dramatically over the past few years that starting with the desktop may be an increasingly backward way of thinking about a web product. Designing for mobile first now can not only open up new opportunities for growth, it can lead to a better overall user experience for a website or application.

Which brings us to our "small" idea. Websites and applications should be designed and built for *mobile first*. Going mobile first:

- Prepares you for the explosive growth and new opportunities emerging on mobile today,
- Forces you to focus and prioritize your products by embracing the constraints inherent in mobile design, and
- Allows you to deliver innovative experiences by building on new capabilities native to mobile devices and modes of use.

In fact, there's enough benefit to a mobile first design approach that it's worth thinking about even if you don't have immediate plans to ship a mobile experience. Just a half-day of brainstorming about your mobile experience can open up new ways of thinking about your product.

But don't just take my word for it. Some of the biggest web companies in the world are adopting a mobile first design philosophy as well. Google Chairman Eric Schmidt advises: "The simple guideline is whatever you are doing—do mobile first," (http://bkaprt.com/mf/1). Kate Aronowitz, Facebook's Director of Design, says "We're just now starting to get into mobile first and then web second for a lot of our products. What we're finding is that the designers on mobile are really embracing the constraints [and] that it's actually teaching us a lot about how to design back to the desktop," (http://bkaprt.com/mf/2). And Kevin Lynch, Adobe's CTO, states: "We really need to shift to think about mobile first....This is a bigger shift than we saw with the personal computing revolution," (http://bkaprt.com/mf/3).

For these organizations and many others like them, mobile first is a big deal. But why is mobile so important and how can you get started designing for it? Well, that's why you're holding a whole book about this small idea in your hands.

About this book

Your time is precious so this book is short and to the point. The first section outlines why a mobile first approach for websites and applications makes sense now. The second section details how designing mobile web experiences is different (from designing desktop web experiences) so you can take what you know about designing for the web and get started on mobile today.

You won't find any code in this book; there are many programmers out there who can provide better advice on mobile development than I can. What you will find is a business case for mobile first and many design patterns and best practices that you can continue coming back to as you design and develop mobile web experiences.

It's also worth pointing out up front that I'm going to use the term "mobile web experience" instead of "mobile web" or "mobile website" throughout this book. Fundamentally, there's just one World Wide Web, but it can be experienced in different ways on different devices. We're focusing on the mobile experience in these pages.

Now I promised conciseness, so let's dispense with the introductions and dive into how going small first can ultimately help you go very, very big.

Part 1

WHY MOBILE FIRST?

Here's the elevator pitch: designing for mobile first not only prepares you for the explosive growth and new opportunities on the mobile internet, it forces you to focus and enables you to innovate in ways you previously couldn't. Of course there's a lot of detail behind that statement, which is what this part is all about.

GROWTH

TAKE A RIDE ON THE SUBWAY, stop by the mall, or go anywhere near a high school and you'll encounter the most recent evolution of the human race. Small, light-emitting plastic screens attached to people's hands are just about anywhere you look. Thankfully, this isn't some odd genetic mutation—it's just our friend, the mobile device. And he's everywhere.

In case you haven't been keeping up with the latest stats, I'll give you a quick recap: mobile is growing like crazy. (Really technical, I know.) While analysts have predicted for years that mobile will be "the next big thing," their prophecies are finally coming true in a very big way. To understand just how big, let's look at some recent statistics:

- Smartphones were boldly predicted to out-ship the combined global market of laptop, desktop, and notebook computers in 2012. They did so in the last quarter of 2010 (http://bkaprt.com/mf/4, PDF; FIG 1.1)—two years earlier than predicted!

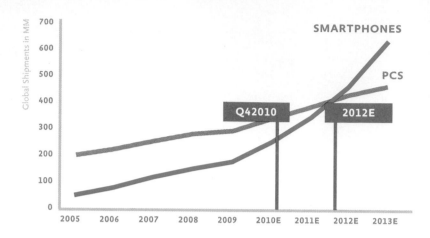

FIG 1.1: Global smartphone shipments surpassed global PC shipments two years earlier than predicted. (Sources: http://bkaprt.com/mf/4)

- That means more people will be using mobile devices to access the web than those getting online with desktops and laptops. This transition has already started. Home usage of personal computers in 2010 was down 20% from 2008 in the United States. The culprit? Smartphones and tablets gobbling up our time online (http://bkaprt.com/mf/5).
- As further proof, consider that in November 2010 visitors to web-based email sites declined 6%, but visitors accessing email with their mobile devices grew by 36% (http://bkaprt.com/mf/6).
- Traffic to mobile websites in 2010 grew 600% after tripling between 2009 and 2010 (http://bkaprt.com/mf/7).
- And it's only going to get bigger. While half a billion people accessed the mobile internet worldwide in 2009, heavy mobile data users will triple to one billion by 2013 (http://bkaprt.com/mf/8; http://bkaprt.com/mf/9, PDF).
- So it's not hard to imagine how another bold prediction like "mobile phones will overtake PCs as the most common web access devices worldwide by 2013" will happen much earlier than predicted as well (http://bkaprt.com/mf/10).

There aren't just a lot more bits flying around on mobile networks. Actual businesses are flourishing on mobile in ecommerce, social, search, and beyond. That's right—real money is being made on mobile, which makes clients and stakeholders take note.

- PayPal is seeing up to $10 million in mobile payment volume per day (http://bkaprt.com/mf/11).
- eBay's global mobile sales generated nearly $2 billion in 2010 (http://bkaprt.com/mf/12).
- Google's mobile searches grew 130% in the third quarter of 2010 (http://bkaprt.com/mf/13).
- Of Pandora's total user base, 50% subscribe to the service on mobile (http://bkaprt.com/mf/12).

And just in case you think your website or application is immune, the average smartphone user visits up to 24 websites a day and the top 50% of websites only account for 40% of all mobile visits (http://bkaprt.com/mf/14). That means your site is very likely a part of the mobile growth story as well.

Truthfully, you don't need all these statistics to realize that mobile use is exploding. You just need to look around you and see how often people are staring at the little screen in their hand. Mobile is already all around us.

SO WHAT CHANGED?

To explain why mobile is on such a tear, I need to take us on a US history lesson all the way back to 2006. If you can't imagine what life was like way back then, let me re-introduce you to the Motorola Z3: a follow-up to the incredibly popular Motorola RAZR phone (FIG 1.2).

The Z3 was a high-end mobile device in the United States in 2006. It featured SMS, email, instant messaging, a two megapixel camera, a music player, a full color screen, and a WAP 2.0/XHTML web browser; it connected to AT&T's EDGE high-speed data network, and the experience of using the web on it...*sucked*.

FIG 1.2: The Motorola Z3 mobile phone was state-of-the-art in the US back in 2006.

Just how bad was it? I counted almost two minutes from starting the web browser to finally seeing a web page that consisted of just a few text links (http://bkaprt.com/mf/15). In a world where websites measure their response times in milliseconds, it's not hard to see how painful that could feel. But it wasn't just the wait; using the phone's keypad to triple-tap text was a chore, and even predictive text tools like T9 (http://bkaprt.com/mf/16) didn't fully ease the pain.

But something happened less than a year later that really changed things. On June 29, 2007, Steve Jobs got on stage and introduced the first iPhone. Apple fanboy or not, it's hard to deny the impact this device has had on the mobile internet. Here was a mobile phone on which browsing the web really did not suck. Looking at AT&T's mobile data traffic from 2006 to 2009 (when it was the exclusive carrier of the iPhone in the US) tells the story quite clearly (**FIG 1.3**).

During this time period, AT&T saw a 4,932% increase in mobile data traffic (http://bkaprt.com/mf/9; PDF)—no wonder their service was spotty for so long! The difference between a device that sucks for browsing the web and one that is great

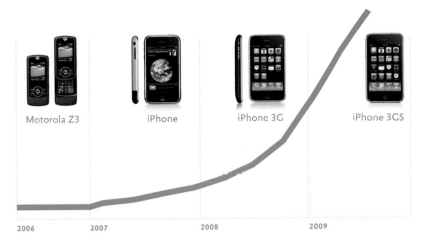

Motorola Z3   iPhone   iPhone 3G   iPhone 3GS

2006   2007   2008   2009

FIG 1.3: AT&T's meteoric rise in mobile data traffic can be seen in more detail at http://bkaprt.com/mf/9 (PDF). (Source: AT&T, Morgan Stanley Research.)

for browsing the web is actually quite significant. In fact, in 2009, one iPhone was responsible for as much mobile traffic as 30 basic feature phones (http://bkaprt.com/mf/17)—no doubt aided by the flat-fee data plan available with the device.

But mobile isn't growing just because devices are getting better: they're getting cheaper as well. People who could never afford a desktop or laptop computer can now get online using inexpensive mobile devices and increasingly affordable data plans.

Broader coverage from faster networks has also been adding fuel to the fire. In 2010 alone, mobile network speeds doubled. As networks became twice as fast, the average amount of data traffic used per smartphone doubled as well. And this use of this data isn't going to stop anytime soon, global mobile data traffic is projected to increase 26-fold between 2010 and 2015 (http://bkaprt.com/mf/17)!

That's a whole lot of opportunity coming your way, really fast.

ALL DEVICES ARE NOT CREATED EQUAL

But before we get ahead of ourselves with pie-in-the-sky mobile web usage fantasies, let's ground things a bit. First, mobile data traffic includes a lot more than just the web. Second, basic feature phones still make up the vast majority of devices on the mobile network and there's a world of difference between feature phone use and usage of more capable mobile devices. Just what kinds of differences are we talking about?

- Of smartphone owners, 35% browse the mobile internet at least daily, versus only 4% of feature phone owners.
- Of smartphone users, 31% have accessed social networks using their mobile browser, compared to only 7% of feature phone users.
- Of smartphone users, 70% have accessed email on their mobile device, versus only 12% of feature phone users.
- And all this was in 2009! Plus this data includes "smart-phones" with painful web browsers as well (http://bkaprt.com/mf/18). So chances are there's an even bigger gap today.

To ensure everyone on the mobile web can access your content now you would need a solution for feature phones, smartphones, and everything in between. But in this book, I'm going to focus mostly on designing for smartphones. Not because Google is giving me a kickback for every Android phone sold, but because:

- Smartphones have a disproportionate amount of web and data usage. According to Cisco, smartphones represent only 13% of total global handsets in use today, but they make up 78% of total handset traffic (source: http://bkaprt.com/mf/19; PDF).
- The rate of smartphone adoption is extremely fast and get-ting faster. In the third quarter of 2010, smartphone sales grew 96% from the previous year. Many more people are getting smartphones every single day (http://bkaprt.com/20).

- With each new volley of devices, smartphones are getting more and more affordable. What previously cost several hundred dollars is now approaching $100 and below; this opens up a huge new market of users.
- So it's not outlandish to suggest that today's smartphone will simply be tomorrow's "phone."

For these reasons and more, smartphones represent a huge opportunity for immediate and long-term customer engagement for many companies. There are, of course, many opportunities with the vast number of feature phones out there today as well—especially through integrated services like SMS and specialized mobile browsers like OperaMini (which does a nice job of bringing better web browsing to feature phones). However, the mobile industry is moving toward smartphones, and so will this book.

But every device labeled a smartphone isn't created equally, either. At the beginning of 2010, iPhone data usage was over four times higher than any other smartphone platform. But by the end of the year, other mobile devices had caught up, and iPhone data usage was only 1.75 times higher than Google's Android platform (http://bkaprt.com/mf/17).

Usage can also change dramatically within a single platform. When Research in Motion (RIM) introduced a more capable web browser with their Storm mobile device, it quickly shot up to 16% of all of RIM's mobile traffic on the Verizon network (http://bkaprt.com/mf/21). The Blackberry devices made by RIM today have an even better web browser so expect usage to grow even more.

These examples not only illustrate the impact a more capable mobile device can have on usage; they also highlight just how quickly things are changing. The rate of innovation in mobile devices is unparalleled; as a result, it's creating all kinds of new opportunities.

With new capabilities come new ways to interact with the web and with digital services, information, and people. We'll talk a lot more about this later in the book, but for now I just want to point out that more capable devices and faster networks don't just amount to more traffic to your site. They introduce entirely new opportunities for engagement as well.

Consider the local review service, Yelp. Their mobile products are used by just 7% of their total audience but are responsible for 35% of all their searches. Every other second Yelp's mobile products manage a call to a local business or a request for driving directions (http://bkaprt.com/mf/22). That's a whole new set of interactions Yelp didn't have before people started using their service on mobile devices.

As another example, let's look at the real estate service, Zillow. Their customers are viewing active listings 45% more often from mobile devices—compared to their desktop website (http://bkaprt.com/mf/23). These are primarily active buyers on location or scoping out neighborhoods; they represent a new kind of audience for the company created by the growth of mobile.

WHAT ABOUT THE NATIVES?

Of course we can't talk about mobile internet growth without mentioning the ongoing debate between native mobile applications and mobile web solutions. While many people try to argue for one side or the other, the truth is there are great reasons for doing both.

Because native mobile applications run, well—natively—they have access to system resources that web applications do not. This means user interface transitions and interactions are generally smoother in native applications. Trying to replicate these effects in the browser can lead to noticeable hiccups and lags in the user experience.

Native mobile applications give you robust access to hardware capabilities that you currently can't get through mobile web browsers. Core features like access to the address book, SMS, camera, audio inputs, and other built-in sensors are mostly unavailable. Also absent is the ability to run processes in the background and easily monetize through mobile app stores or in-app purchases. Non-native applications can't get into a native app store and have a much harder time getting on

FIG 1.4: Even though they have native mobile applications for iOS, Android, Blackberry, and Palm, the location-based service Gowalla also has a mobile web experience for anyone following links to Gowalla on their mobile device.

the home screen of people's mobile devices, which can negatively impact discovery and ongoing usage.

So if your mobile product or business requires deeper hardware access, background processes, app or in-app sales, or more integrated placement on mobile devices to be viable, you may need a native solution. But that doesn't mean you don't need a mobile web solution, too.

As mobile strategist Jason Grigsby is fond of pointing out, "Web links don't open apps, they go to web pages," (http://bkaprt.com/mf/24). Whether it's through search, email, social networks, or on web pages, if you have content online, people will find and share links to it. Not having a mobile web solution means anyone that follows those links on a mobile device won't have a great experience (if they can even access your content at all). Having a native mobile application won't help (FIG 1.4).

Access might even be the biggest user benefit for a mobile web experience. Even if you build a native mobile application for one platform, chances are you won't be able to create one for every platform. Apple's iOS requires Objective C; Google's Android needs Java; Microsoft's Windows Phone 7 relies on

Silverlight; Samsung's Bada requires C++; RIM's Blackberry has Java, WebWorks, and Adobe Air solutions. Finding a company that can build something for all of these technologies is rare. And even if you can create native applications for each platform, the cost of maintaining them can quickly make it prohibitive.

Plus the web might be your most popular mobile experience anyway. Fourteen percent of Twitter's members use the mobile web experience compared to 8% using the native iPhone app and 7% using the Blackberry native app. The rest of Twitter's native mobile applications are each used by less than 4% of their user base (http://bkaprt.com/mf/25).

The same pattern can be found on Facebook. Close to 19% of Facebook posts are created on the mobile web experience, while Facebook's native iPhone, Android, and Blackberry apps only account for about 4% of posts each (http://bkaprt.com/mf/26). It turns out access (anywhere) goes a long way.

In fact, native mobile applications are actually increasing web use on mobile devices. Each time a web link is shared or referenced in a native application it opens in a web browser window. So more native application use quickly turns into more web use.

Mobile web experiences also don't require users to download updates (a fix on the server is a fix on the site), and they enable you to do frequent A/B (or bucket) testing of multiple design options. If either of those considerations is of vital importance to you, a mobile web application can make more sense.

But perhaps the best reason to start with a mobile web solution is that it builds on web design and development skills you already have. You don't have to wait to get started. In fact, I think you should start right away.

THE TIME IS NOW

Fueled by capable devices and faster networks, mobile internet usage is exploding. Building mobile first not only positions you to take advantage of this growth, it also opens up new opportunities for engaging your customers.

This isn't just an opportunity to create a mobile version of your web product; it's an opportunity to provide an improved overall experience for your customers.

Consider the social networking service Facebook. There are more than 250 million active users (http://bkaprt.com/mf/27) accessing Facebook through their mobile devices. These users are twice as active on Facebook as non-mobile users.

The combination of mobile and desktop experiences results in more engaged users across both sets of devices. That's because Facebook doesn't just think of its mobile experience as a part of the desktop site; it embraces it as a way to make the entire Facebook experience better.

In the words of Joe Hewitt, former lead developer of Facebook's iPhone application: "My goal was initially just to make a mobile companion, but I became convinced it was possible to create a version of Facebook that was actually better than the website," (http://bkaprt.com/mf/28). That's really the mobile opportunity in a nutshell.

Now—how do the constraints and capabilities of mobile devices help get us there?

2 CONSTRAINTS

WHILE IT'S TRUE the incredible growth of the mobile internet has been fueled by better and better devices, mobile still remains a very constrained environment. Screens are small, networks are unreliable, and people can find themselves in all kinds of situations when they pull out their mobile devices. But these constraints are not only good for business, they're good for design as well.

This is especially true if you subscribe to the adage that design is the process of gradually applying constraints until an elegant solution remains. In other words, embracing constraints (rather than fighting them) will ultimately get you to better designs.

SCREEN SIZE

Though the topic of available screen real estate on the desktop was hotly contested for many years in the web design community, we finally settled on 1024×768 pixels as our beachhead. Today, mobile takes our sunny beach and cuts it down to little more than a sandbox.

The first volley of smartphones running iOS, Android, and WebOS mostly stuck to a 320×480 pixel resolution, which meant 80% of the screen space from the desktop was missing. So 80% of the links, ads, text, images, and more from our desktop designs had to find a new home or disappear altogether. There simply wasn't room for them on a mobile screen. And that's...*terrific.*

When you consider the amount of useless navigation, content fluff, and irrelevant promotions that litter a typical web experience, you realize why the mobile diet can be good for both businesses and customers. Once people use the mobile version, it's not uncommon for them to pine for the desktop version to be "that simple."

To see why, let's look at the Southwest Airlines website (**FIG 2.1**), which seems to exemplify the everything-including-the-kitchen-sink problem. Adding things to a website is relatively easy so lots of things get added—especially when multiple stakeholders are involved.

Different internal departments, feature owners, businesses, and individuals have different requirements for websites. So web teams are often left trying to balance many promotions, interactions, content modules, navigation options and more in a single layout. On a 1024×768 screen there are lots of pixels to fill!

The mobile experience (in this case, Southwest's native iPhone application), on the other hand, has a laser-like focus on what customers need and what Southwest does: book travel, check in, check flight status, check miles, and get alerts (**FIG 2.2**). No room for anything else. Only what matters most.

Losing that much screen space forces teams to focus. You have to make sure that what stays on the screen is the most important set of features for your customers and your business. There simply isn't room for any interface debris or content of questionable value. You need to know what matters most.

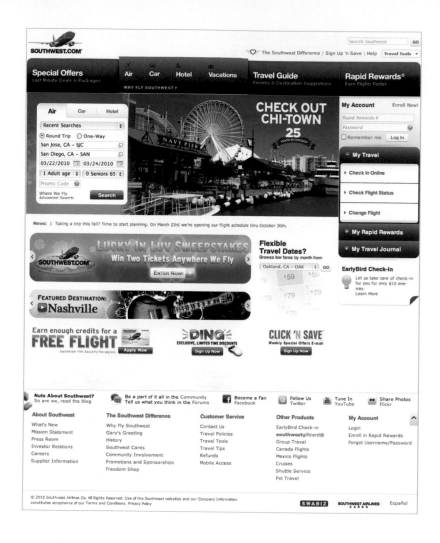

FIG 2.1: The Southwest Airlines website makes sure every pixel is filled with competing messages and calls to action.

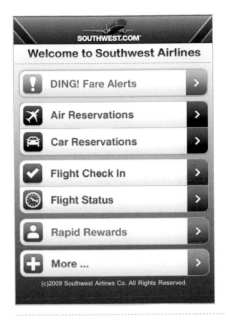

FIG 2.2: The Southwest Airlines iPhone application only has room for what actually matters.

In order to do that you need to really know your customers and your business. Designing for mobile forces you to get there, like it or not.

To further illustrate this point, let's look at the popular photo-sharing site, Flickr. While you may be familiar with Flickr, chances are you are not familiar with all of it. Over the years, the site has grown to boast over 60 navigation options in its top menu alone (**FIG 2.3**).

When it came time to design their mobile web experience, the Flickr team was able to focus these 60 plus options into six. How did they do it? By knowing what their customers did on the site and why. Most Flickr users like to check in and see what's happening with their photos; see new photos from people they know; and explore interesting images from across the site. The mobile website put the focus on these key actions front and center (**FIG 2.4**).

If you design for mobile first, you can create agreement up front on what matters most. You can then apply the same rationale to the desktop (and any other) experience of your

FIG 2.3: All of Flickr's top-level menu options—all at once.

web product. If you can agree on the most important set of features and content for your customers and business, why should that prioritization change with more screen space?

There are, of course, differences based on mobile and desktop usage patterns; but the core value of a web service remains the same across both formats and beyond. In fact, you'll quickly find your customers will expect to do just about everything (within reason) on mobile. Especially those who primarily (or only) use their mobiles to get online. So don't dumb things down on mobile—focus on what really matters most anywhere people can access your website.

With mobile first, the end result is an experience focused on the key tasks users want to accomplish without the extraneous detours and general interface debris that litter many of today's websites. There simply isn't room in a 320×480 pixel screen for elements of questionable value.

PERFORMANCE

Though people try to use their mobile devices just about everywhere (yes, there too!), mobile networks aren't always there to support them. Even when they are, coverage can be expensive (depending on your data plan) and spotty—leading to slower connections and longer, frustrating wait times.

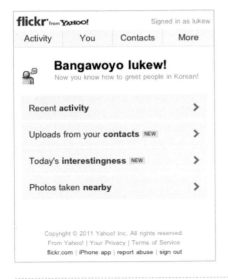

FIG 2.4: Flickr's mobile web experience takes 60 plus navigation options down to six.

Designing for mobile means designing for this reality. Anything that can be done to increase performance on mobile should be done. At the highest level that means sending less stuff and using whichever browser and server technologies are available to you to speed things up and reduce people's monthly carrier bills.

You can require mobile users to download less by managing both the size and number of files (and thereby HTTP requests) you are sending to a device. On mobile devices, each HTTP request can be more costly because of mobile network latency. So make sure you:

- Use image sprites to group multiple images into a single encoded file. (Just make sure it's not too big when decoded!)
- Bundle together and minify CSS and JavaScript files.
- Limit or remove dependencies on heavy JavaScript libraries—especially if they are just being used for one or two functions.
- Likewise, limit the use of CSS grid systems.
- Use proper HTTP headers to ensure files are appropriately cached in the browser's memory.

- Where appropriate, take advantage of modern browser capabilities like Canvas (http://bkaprt.com/mf/29) and Appcache (http://bkaprt.com/mf/30) in HTML5.
- And my favorite: use CSS3 properties for rounded corners, gradients, text shadows, and box shadows. This reduces the need for images across your entire site, keeps things looking great in modern mobile browsers, and provides a decent fallback for browsers that don't support CSS3 well. Just don't go overboard with heavy CSS3 effects, as too many items for the browser to render could actually hurt performance.

Speed isn't just important on mobile. Testing done by Amazon, Yahoo!, Microsoft, and others has consistently shown that even very small delays (100ms) on the desktop can turn users away. Long-term studies by Google found that slow performance has lasting effects, reducing people's activity for five weeks even after a delay has been repaired (http://bkaprt.com/mf/31). So performance matters on the desktop, too.

If you focus on mobile first and make things fast enough for spotty mobile networks, your websites and applications will be blazingly fast on the desktop and your customers will love you for it—just another advantage to embracing mobile constraints up front.

TIME AND PLACE

In its simplest form, context is the circumstances under which something happens. For example, desktop computers are most often used at a desk (in an office or home); with a persistent connection to power and the network; in relative privacy; from a seated position; and so on. While someone can certainly use a mobile device for a long period of time while seated at a desk, there is a much wider set of circumstances possible because mobile devices are naturally portable.

Since mobile devices are (just about) always with their owners, location and time play a big role in how they are used. And that context has a big impact on design. When you design for mobile you are designing something that can be used anywhere and anytime.

Location

When many people first imagine designing for mobile, they picture a hurried businessman on the street. While that can be a real use case to consider, the places where mobile devices are frequently used are much more diverse. A recent survey (http://bkaprt.com/mf/32) looked at where people used their smartphones and found:

- 84% use them at home,
- 80% use them during miscellaneous downtime throughout the day,
- 74% use them while waiting in lines or waiting for appointments,
- 69% use them while shopping,
- 64% use them at work,
- 62% use them while watching TV (a different study claims 84%), and
- 47% use them during their commute.

The fact that 84% of people used their mobile device at home is telling. Catching a quick glance at your email at home is perhaps a bigger part of the mobile story than our businessman on the go. What both situations have in common, though, is that we're unlikely to get someone's full attention.

When reflecting on a lot of mobile usage patterns, I like to imagine people as "one eyeball and one thumb." One thumb because they are likely to be holding their mobile in one hand and using a single thumb to control it; one eyeball because in many locations where mobile devices are used we only have people's partial attention.

They're waiting in line and sneaking a peek at a sports score; they have a baby on one arm and their mobile in the other; they are on a crowded subway on the way to work; or they are lounging on the couch with the TV running in the

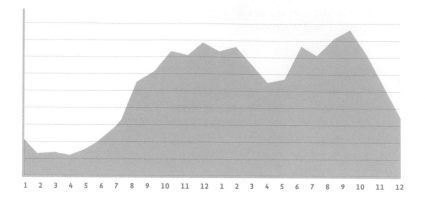

FIG 2.5: When people are reading saved articles on their computer (http://bkaprt.com/mf/33).

background. Thinking "one eyeball, one thumb" forces you to simplify mobile designs so they can be understood and used in these kinds of situations and more.

Even in distraction-free environments where focused use is possible, a simplified mobile experience goes a long way to making people feel comfortable and relaxed.

Time

While people can technically use their computers at any time, there are different periods of time during the day when different devices come out more often. To illustrate, the graph in **FIG 2.5** shows the number of articles Read It Later users read each hour on their desktop and laptop computers. The number of reads grows more sharply until noon and then begins to fall off until after work (6–9 p.m.).

The second graph shows the number of articles read by iPhone users each hour (**FIG 2.6**). There are four major peaks: 6 a.m. (breakfast); 9 a.m. (the morning commute and start of workday); 5 p.m.–6 p.m. (end of the work day and the commute home); 8 p.m.–10 p.m. (couch time, prime time, bed time).

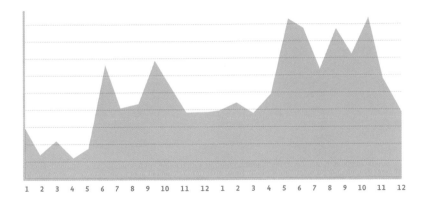

1 2 3 4 5 6 7 8 9 10 11 12 1 2 3 4 5 6 7 8 9 10 11 12

FIG 2.6: When people are reading saved articles on their iPhone (http://bkaprt.com/mf/33).

Clearly computer time is not mobile time. Nor is it tablet time. To further illustrate how different devices can impact website or application usage, we can look at when people are reading Read It Later articles on their iPad (**FIG 2.7**). While there is a small spike in the morning and steady use throughout the day, the bulk of iPad reading happens in the evening— in bed. I swear I'm just reading web design articles!

So different devices often do come out at different times. In some cases, it's just a matter of proximity. What's the closest device I can use to get what I need done? In many other cases, though, it's because different devices are better suited to specific types of tasks. This becomes clear when you look at computer and mobile usage together in one chart (**FIG 2.8**).

This chart does a nice job of illustrating that people often use their mobile devices in shorter bursts (that's why the peaks are sharper) throughout the day. Rachel Hinman at Nokia has a great analogy that contrasts mobile behavior with desktop behavior; she says the desktop is "diving" while mobile is "snorkeling" (http://bkaprt.com/mf/34).

Web applications that align well with shorter, burst-like behavior by providing their customers with quick, up-to-date, and highly relevant updates throughout the day are growing like weeds on mobile. Access to Facebook through mobile

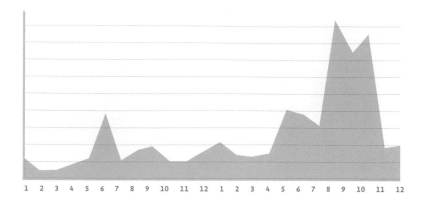

| 1 | 2 | 3 | 4 | 5 | 6 | 7 | 8 | 9 | 10 | 11 | 12 | 1 | 2 | 3 | 4 | 5 | 6 | 7 | 8 | 9 | 10 | 11 | 12 |

FIG 2.7: When people are reading saved articles on their iPad (http://bkaprt.com/mf/33).

browsers grew 112% in one year. Access to Twitter through mobile browsers experienced a 347% jump in just one year (http://bkaprt.com/mf/18). Both of these services are perfect for snorkeling in a sea of your friends' status updates.

But note that in both diving and snorkeling, you're looking at fish underwater. While the time and place people interact with mobile may be different, the core value of your website stays the same. So once again, don't deny people content and features just because they're on a mobile device.

EMBRACING CONSTRAINTS

Mobile comes with a natural set of constraints that may at first seem limiting. Screens are small, connections are slow, and people often only give you their partial attention or short bursts of their time. Designing for mobile first forces you to embrace these constraints to develop an elegant mobile-appropriate solution. But the benefits go well beyond mobile.

Small screen sizes force you to prioritize what really matters to your customers and business. There simply isn't room for anything else. Slow connections and limited data plans require you to be vigilant about performance, resulting in fast-loading websites everywhere.

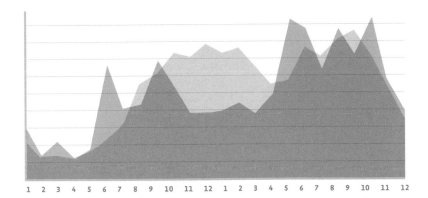

1 2 3 4 5 6 7 8 9 10 11 12 1 2 3 4 5 6 7 8 9 10 11 12

FIG 2.8: Super-imposing when people read saved articles on their computer with when they read them on their iPhone (http://bkaprt.com/mf/33).

Location and time act as constraints on the mobile design process because they force you to think differently about how people will use your products throughout their day. They also create new opportunities for engagement that can help you innovate. So let's talk about the new things mobile allows you to do.

3 CAPABILITIES

THE NATURAL CONSTRAINTS of mobile devices, networks, and usage patterns help focus and simplify mobile experiences. But designing for mobile isn't just about embracing limitations—it's also about extending what you can do.

People can (and do) use their mobile devices anywhere and everywhere. That opens up new ways for us to meet customer needs and business goals. When these opportunities come together with the technical capabilities now present in many mobile devices, lots of innovative experiences can emerge.

Since that sounds like something a corporate PowerPoint presentation would say, let me illustrate the idea with a story.

FINDING THE TUBE

When I was last in London, I wanted to take in a few sights. Having been there before, I knew the London Underground (or Tube) was the best way to move around, but I didn't know where to find the stations closest to me. Solving this problem

FIG 3.1: The Transport for London website's home page

on my laptop only required a quick search that dropped me off on the London Transport site (**FIG 3.1**).

Once here, I easily found a link to the Tube map and arrived on a web page dedicated to "Maps" with a link to the "Standard Tube Map."

Now let me pause here for a moment and point out that a lot of web usability and information architecture best practices have been applied to the London Transport site (**FIG 3.2**). It's clear what's a link, large images provide visual cues about each section, and the links have even been annotated with PDF icons and file sizes to let you know what's behind them. I'm also sure they thought a lot about how to organize the

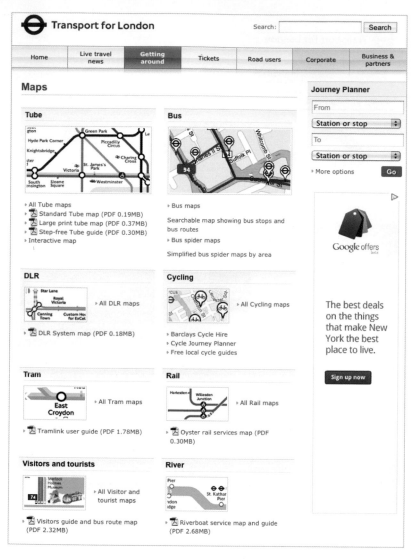

FIG 3.2: Years of web design best practices at work on the Maps page.

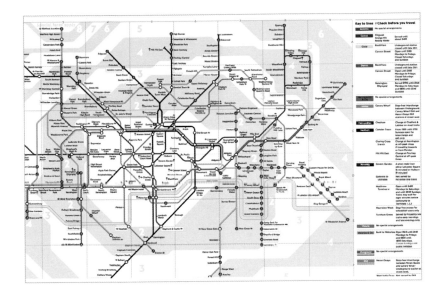

FIG 3.3: The PDF of the Tube map that ended my search.

various pages on the site and how people could move between them. So it wasn't very hard for me to find the right information and access the PDF map of the Tube (**FIG 3.3**).

Now let's contrast this experience of finding nearby Tube stations on the desktop by doing the same thing using a native mobile application called Nearest Tube. Nearest Tube uses a few mobile device capabilities to deliver a very different experience. In particular, it relies on access to a mobile's location detection services, digital compass (or magnetometer), video camera, and accelerometer.

Location detection finds your position on a map, a digital compass determines the direction you are facing, and the video camera allows you to display digital information over your current field of view. So the experience of finding the nearest Tube station using Nearest Tube consists of opening the application and just looking at the screen (**FIG 3.4**).

Overlaid on your current view of the world are markers pointing to the Tube stations closest to you, the routes they

FIG 3.4: The Nearest Tube application points out stations near you using a mobile device's video camera and digital compass (http://bkaprt.com/mf/35).

service, and how far away from you they are. The application also uses an accelerometer (a sensor that measures how the device is moving) to change the information you see depending on where you point the camera. Position it in front of you and you see more detailed information about nearby stations; lift it up higher and get the same information about stations further away (**FIG 3.5**).

Now I'm not suggesting this mobile "augmented experience" is better than the desktop web one we just walked through—because, frankly, both have usability issues. But, wow is this different. The desktop website and this mobile application solve the same user need in dramatically different ways.

Nearest Tube uses mobile device capabilities (camera, location detection, magnetometer, and accelerometer) to really innovate in what seems to be a simple use case. And this is what mobile capabilities allow you to do: reinvent ways to meet people's needs using exciting new tools that are now at your disposal.

Looking down

Looking ahead   **Looking up**

FIG 3.5: Nearest Tube provides different information depending on how you position your mobile device.

BUT WHAT'S IN THE BROWSER?

Before we get ahead of ourselves, not everything that Nearest Tube has done in their native mobile application is currently possible in all mobile web browsers. Half the capabilities we just saw used (location detection and device orientation) are mostly available, while the other half (video camera and magnetometer) are mostly *not* available in smartphone web browsers at the time of this writing. So (as I pointed out earlier) there are still reasons to build experiences natively. But if you consider the glass half full, there are a lot of interesting new capabilities available in mobile web browsers, and more are being added all the time.

It's also worth pointing out that the most important opportunities come from people's needs and not from any specific hardware features. Technical capabilities can help us meet these needs in new and interesting ways, but building things just because we can usually doesn't help our customers.

Location detection

On the desktop, we can be about 99% sure we know the country a visitor to our website is in. While that has its uses, it doesn't really give us much to work with. Most smartphones, on the other hand, have several ways to detect someone's location that can be accessed from within the browser. **TABLE 3.1** (assembled by Rahul Nair) provides a quick overview of the techniques at our disposal.

While cell towers can be used to locate a modern feature phone, a device like the iPhone relies on WiFi beacons two-thirds to three-quarters of the time it locates itself. WiFi beacons (based on where WiFi hotspots are located) work indoors, don't use up additional battery life, and can find locations almost instantly. GPS units have problems on all three fronts, but they have much higher location accuracy. When you need a foolproof location, GPS and cell towers are a much surer bet.

But don't worry too much about these issues. The web browsers that provide location APIs will simply give you the most accurate location information they have from the device when you ask for it.

Location detection is a big deal because it allows mobile web experiences to use your current whereabouts to deliver relevant information like the nearest movie theater or restaurant, local weather, traffic information, digital artifacts (like photos or comments) left by others, and more. Your current location can also be used to set smart defaults in search results or to customize actions or options based on where you are (**FIG 3.6-3.7**).

	ACCURACY	POSITIONING TIME	BATTERY LIFE
GPS	10m	2–10 minutes (only indoors)	5–6 hours on most phones
WiFi	50m (improves with density)	Almost instant (server connect and lookup)	No additional effect
Cell tower triangulation	100–1400m (based on density)	Almost instant (server connect and lookup)	Negligible
Single cell tower	500–2500m (based on density)	Almost instant (server connect and lookup)	Negligible
IP	Country: 99% City: 46% US, 53% International Zip: 0%	Almost instant (server connect and lookup)	Negligible

TABLE 3.1: An overview of the different ways a modern mobile device can detect your location. Smartphones make hybrid use of GPS, WiFi, and cell tower triangulation; laptops and desktops use WiFi, IP, and only rarely GPS.

FIG 3.6: Kayak's mobile web experience allows you to search for hotels using your current location.

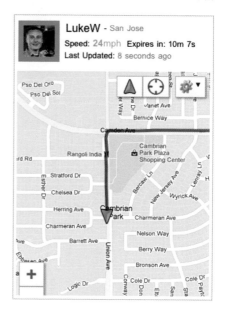

FIG 3.7: Glympse's mobile web experience allows you to see how far away someone is from you and how long it will take them to arrive.

FIG 3.8: Flipping the Android Gmail application to landscape mode gives you more room to compose your email message.

As we saw earlier, the presence of accurate location information can create new kinds of uses for your service. Every other second, someone using Yelp on his or her mobile device calls a local business. People are viewing 20,000 homes an hour using Zillow on mobile. The opportunities for services to take advantage of location information are huge.

Device orientation/accelerometer

Because of the size of desktop monitors and laptops, we're not prone to moving them around a whole lot. Mobile devices are different. They fit in the palm of our hand so they can easily be pivoted, rotated, and moved. Accelerometers let us know when that happens so our websites and applications can respond accordingly.

The simplest use of an accelerometer is to detect when a mobile device has been turned to be viewed horizontally or vertically (http://bkaprt.com/mf/36). This little bit of knowledge can be used to make small or dramatic changes to an application.

Tilt scrolling

FIG 3.9: Tilt scrolling in Instapaper allows you to read articles at your own pace without having to touch the screen.

When you enable Tilt Scrolling, you can automatically scroll up and down by tilting your iPhone slightly forward or back.

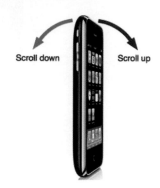

Scroll down   Scroll up

In their native email application on Android, Google takes advantage of this orientation change to give people more room to write when composing an email. If the device is flipped to horizontal mode, a wider text area appears for the message and a "Done" button appears on the right (**FIG 3.8**).

Without this design change, rotating this mobile device horizontally would have made typing an email harder. There would be less room and more text fields. But instead Google has provided people with more room—thereby turning a potential limitation into a benefit.

Accelerometers can also tell us the rate at which a device is moving in someone's hand. This one capability can take a common task on the web and make it easier and fun. Consider the act of reading an article online: every day, millions of people skim the top paragraph and perhaps scroll down using their mouse, or click on a scrollbar in their browser. Not really much to innovate right?

Once again, though, we see the capabilities in mobile devices outpacing what we can do on the desktop. For example,

FIG 3.10: Just shake your iPhone to make it snow in this robot's globe (http://bkaprt.com/mf/37).

the reading service Instapaper allows you to save articles to read later on your mobile device (and many other devices as well). Instapaper's iPhone application uses accelerometer data to gradually scroll text in an article for you as you tilt the phone—no scrolling needed (**FIG 3.9**). You can even tilt the device more or less to read at your own pace. So even the most common tasks online can be rethought given mobile capabilities.

Astute readers will note that these last two examples were native applications and not mobile web applications. So to balance the tide, let's look at two uses of device orientation in the web browser.

FIG 3.11: Move your mobile device in any direction to pan these images 360 degrees (http://bkaprt.com/mf/38).

The first one recreates the venerable snow globe—digitally. Just shake your phone to make the flakes come down in the web browser (**FIG 3.10**).

The second example goes a bit further and uses an iPhone 4's gyroscope (which detects 360 degrees of motion) to make it easy to pan large photos simply by moving the phone in your hand (**FIG 3.11**).

Touch

Interface designers have always lauded direct manipulation. After all, why bother with a mouse and keyboard when you can just reach out and touch something? Touch-enabled mobile devices allow us to interact with the web using our fingers—that's wide-open terrain for new interactions that just "feel" right.

The next section of this book is going to cover how to make sure people can use your websites on touch-enabled mobile devices, so for now I'd just like to highlight that touch is a capability ripe for innovation. We're only beginning to

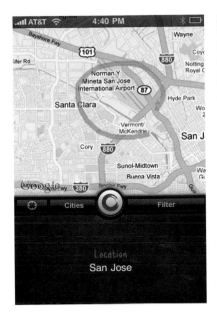

FIG 3.12: Yahoo!'s Sketch a Search application allows you to search by drawing lines and circles on a map.

explore how touch gestures can be used to manage, create, and access information on the web. From simple actions like "pull down to refresh" and "swipe for more options," new interactions are slowly becoming expectations.

But touch can go beyond simple interactions and sometimes drive the entire way an application is used. Consider the Sketch a Search native mobile application from Yahoo!. To find a spot to eat near you, just draw a circle or line on the map using your finger (**FIG 3.12**).

Results come back within or along the shape you've drawn. Compared to the standard desktop web approach of typing in a location and search term, letting your fingers do the searching is not only easy but fun as well.

EXTENDING YOUR CAPABILITIES

When you design and develop for mobile first, you can use exciting new capabilities on the web to create innovative ways of meeting people's needs. Technical capabilities like location detection, device orientation, and touch are available on many mobile web browsers today. And additional capabilities may be here soon, including:

- *Direction:* from a digital compass
- *Gyroscope:* 360 degrees of motion
- *Audio:* input from a microphone; output to speaker
- *Video and image:* capture and input from a camera
- *Dual cameras:* front and back
- *Device connections:* through Bluetooth
- *Proximity:* device closeness to physical objects
- *Ambient light:* light/dark environment awareness
- *NFC:* Near Field Communications through RFID readers

Starting with mobile puts these capabilities in your hands now so you can rethink how people can interact with your website and the world around them. As mobile web browsers continue to gain access to capabilities currently reserved only for native mobile applications, these opportunities will only increase.

STARTING MOBILE FIRST

At this point we've talked about reasons for designing and developing web experiences for mobile first. A mobile first approach:

- Prepares you for the explosive growth and new opportunities emerging on mobile today.
- Forces you to focus and prioritize your products by embracing the constraints inherent in mobile design.
- Allows you to deliver innovative experiences by building on new capabilities native to mobile devices.

Hopefully you're convinced that mobile web experiences are not only a great opportunity for growth, but also offer new ways of meeting your customer's needs as well. If so, you might be thinking, "Ok, but how do I get started?" Well, I'm glad you asked.

Part 2

HOW TO GO MOBILE

It's clear that mobile is an exciting new opportunity for many of us. But if you're coming from a desktop web design background, how do you make the transition to designing mobile web experiences? While a lot of your existing tools, experiences, and skills will still apply, you'll probably want to start thinking a bit differently about organization, actions, inputs, and layout on mobile.

In the next part, we're going to dispense with introducing the basic concepts behind web design and just highlight where and why designing for mobile is different. So you can take what you already know and get going.

4 ORGANIZATION

WHEN IT COMES TO ORGANIZING the content and actions on mobile, solid information architecture principles like clear labeling, balanced breadth and depth, and appropriate mental models remain important. But the organization of mobile web experiences also needs to:

- Align with how people use their mobile devices and why.
- Emphasize content over navigation.
- Provide relevant options for exploration and pivoting.
- Maintain clarity and focus.

ALIGN WITH MOBILE BEHAVIORS

In the previous part, we talked about the constraints and capabilities that make designing for mobile unique. Similarly, the desktop web also has a set of limitations and possibilities that make it distinct. So simply porting over what worked for you on the desktop to mobile often doesn't make sense. Instead, you need to think about what mobile is uniquely good at and align it with the needs of your customers.

Looking at this intersection at a high level can illuminate how people are typically using their mobile devices and why. In his book *Tapworthy*, author Josh Clark focused on three critical mobile behaviors: micro-tasking, "I'm local," and "I'm bored." These align pretty well with Google's breakdown of mobile users into three behavioral groups: urgent now, repetitive now, and bored now. Regardless of how you chose to label these behaviors, mobile usage generally consists of a couple of interaction types:

- *Lookup/Find (urgent info, local):* I need an answer to something now—frequently related to my current location in the world.
- *Explore/Play (bored, local):* I have some time to kill and just want a few idle time distractions.
- *Check In/Status (repeat/micro-tasking):* Something important to me keeps changing or updating and I want to stay on top of it.
- *Edit/Create (urgent change/micro-tasking):* I need to get something done now that can't wait.

Because they directly align with why people pull out their mobile devices, these behaviors often determine how your mobile experience can be structured and organized to meet people's needs. For example, the Flickr photo sharing mobile web experience has four primary actions. Recent activity and uploads from your contacts let people check-in on what's new with their friends and photos; today's interestingness and photos taken nearby give people a way to fill idle time by looking at great pictures (FIG 4.1).

Similarly, the Basecamp project management mobile web experience emphasizes the ability to check-in, edit, and create new messages, to-dos, and more. While people's reasons for using Flickr and Basecamp are different, both sites have thought through how they'll be used on mobile and adjusted their organization accordingly.

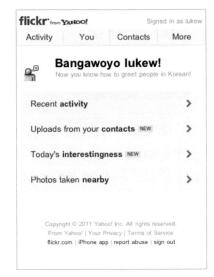
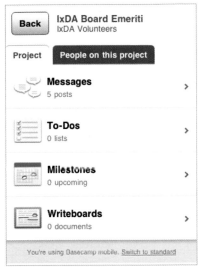

FIG 4.1: Both Flickr and Basecamp's mobile web experiences align with why people pull out their mobile devices.

Aligning with mobile behaviors also naturally aligns your website with real-world needs. Since a mobile experience can be accessed anywhere and everywhere, you need to think through how it can be useful to people wherever they may be. That means lots of real-world use cases that ground your site's organization in what people actually want to do.

I recently found a great example of this in action. On the Mobile in Higher Ed blog (http://bkaprt.com/mf/39), Dave Olsen responded to an xkcd comic (**FIG 4.2**) with:

> ...as I was looking at the right side of the Venn diagram I thought, "That looks like a lot of the current and planned content for our mobile site." [...] removing unnecessary fluff and cruft to fit in the constraints of both the device real estate as well as network limitations, helps craft a better and more useful user experience.

I couldn't have said it better myself.

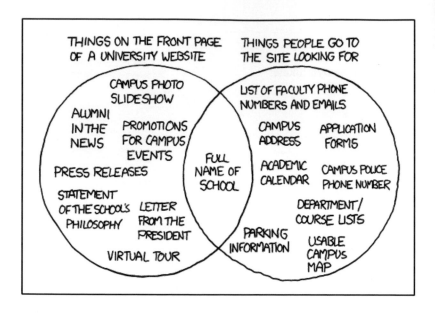

FIG 4.2: A comic from xkcd parodying what people want on a university website versus what they find (http://bkaprt.com/mf/40).

CONTENT OVER NAVIGATION

As a general rule, content takes precedence over navigation on mobile. Whether people are checking on frequently updated data like stocks, news, or scores; looking up local information; or finding their way to articles through search or communication tools—they want immediate answers to their needs and not your site map.

Too many mobile web experiences (like the Flickr and Basecamp examples we just looked at) start the conversation off with a list of navigation options instead of content. Time is often precious on mobile and downloads can cost money, so get people to what they came for as soon as you can.

The YouTube and ESPN mobile web experiences do just that. A simple header tells you whose site you are on and relegates navigation options to a single action. The rest of the

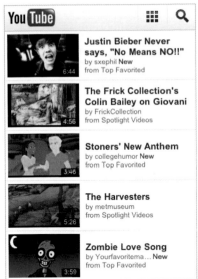

FIG 4.3: ESPN and YouTube's mobile web experiences put the focus on content instead of navigation.

page is filled with timely content to check-in on (ESPN) and popular time killers to explore (YouTube) (FIG 4.3).

PIVOT AND EXPLORE

But wait—if content always takes precedence over navigation, how can I find my way around mobile web experiences? Don't we need a way to navigate and discover what's available? Of course, but allowing people to explore and pivot to relevant content doesn't have to mean piles of navigation bars that bury content.

For example, it's great that Facebook puts relevant content I can frequently check-in on front and center in their mobile web experience; but because of the three navigation bars at the top of their pages, I can only see one update on my screen. The Google Finance mobile web experience also has relevant, timely content—but it's sandwiched below five navigation

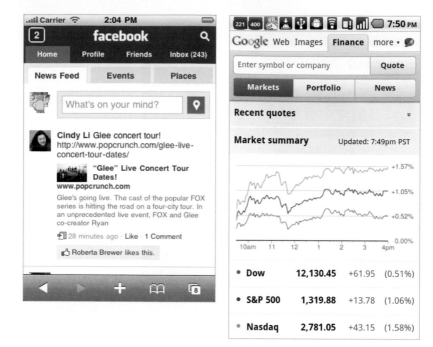

FIG 4.4: Facebook and Google Finance fill precious space with lots of navigation options in their mobile web experience.

bars. That's a lot of precious screen space spent on navigation options people might not need—space that could have been devoted to useful content instead (**FIG 4.4**).

Facebook recently redesigned their mobile web experience and actually reduced the number of navigation options (**FIG 4.5**). If you don't count the Top News and Most Recent filters on their news feed, they cut the number of navigation choices in half (from ten to five). That's a pretty good start!

The examples from YouTube and ESPN (**FIG 4.3**) both emphasize content over navigation, but they handle the ability to pivot and explore the rest of their site through navigation differently. YouTube provides a shortcut to a full screen experience dedicated to getting around the site (**FIG 4.6**). This approach requires you to actively seek out navigation options

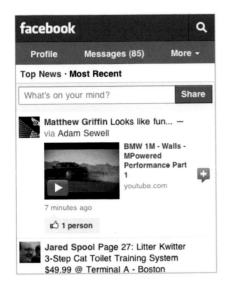

FIG 4.5: Facebook's recent redesign cut down on the number of navigation options in their mobile web experience.

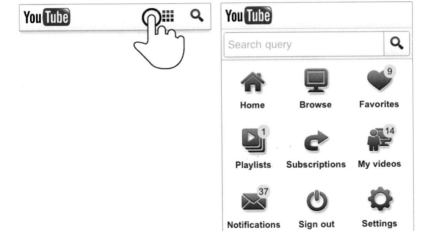

FIG 4.6: YouTube's mobile web experience includes a full page of navigation options accessible from the header.

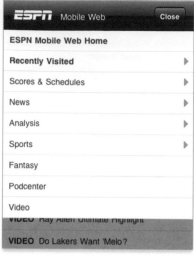

FIG 4.7: ESPN's mobile web experience includes navigation options in the header and at the bottom of every page.

and takes you out of context (to a separate page) when you do. You also need to know that the grid icon in YouTube's header means "navigation menu, please."

ESPN has a more clearly labeled "Menu" button in their header that reveals an extensive (and multi-leveled) navigation list directly below it (**FIG 4.7**). This approach allows you to stay on the current page when considering where to go next. No need to move to and load a separate page. ESPN also repeats their navigation options in a menu at the bottom of most pages.

Controls at the bottom of the screen are easier to interact with one-handed and present people with choices and ideas on what to do next when they get to the end of a screen. YouTube's design lacks these pivots at the end of their pages; when you get to the bottom, there's nowhere left to go (**FIG 4.8**).

Though bottom menus are useful for further exploration, they probably shouldn't just duplicate a menu that can be found elsewhere. Instead, a top-level menu button can simply link people to a navigation list on the bottom of a mobile web-page (after the content). We recently used this approach on the Bagcheck mobile web experience (**FIG 4.9**).

A simple anchor link in the site's header jumps people to navigation options at the bottom of the page. Having this list present at the bottom of content pages allows people to pivot and explore other parts of the site. Especially when they come directly to a content page and may not be familiar with the rest of what the site offers.

The menu on the bottom of Bagcheck pages also has a "top" link to bring people back up to the start of a page if they want to return to the content they were just viewing.

This design uses a minimum amount of navigation elements (just a single link at the top), gives people an opportunity to pivot and explore when they get to the end of content, doesn't duplicate the content of another menu, and (best of all) only requires a simple anchor link to work. That's right: no fancy JavaScript, overlays, or separate navigation pages to maintain—just an anchor that links to the bottom of the page.

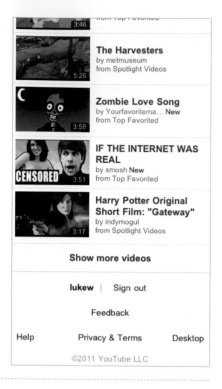

FIG 4.8: The options at the end of a page on YouTube's mobile web experience are basically a dead end. Sign out? Send feedback?

That's like HTML 0. (Which I've heard works in most browsers except Internet Explorer.)

Content pages on Bagcheck also have unique related navigation lists for deeper exploration (**FIG 4.10**). These navigation options allow people to immerse themselves in further information about a single topic if they choose. Or they can simply use the global navigation options below to pivot to a different area of the site.

Contextual navigation options are also useful for tasks. In the Gmail mobile web experience (**FIG 4.11**), a contextual menu of actions can be accessed from the top of the screen. Because these actions are directly related to the current email message being shown, putting them at the bottom of a web page wouldn't be very efficient. Instead, they are always present at the top and thereby instantly accessible.

FIG 4.9: An anchor link in the Bagcheck header jumps you to the site's navigation menu at the bottom of the page.

GETTING BACK

It's always interesting to see how design solutions migrate across digital borders. For example, many native iPhone applications have prominent "back" links in their navigation header (FIG 4.12). Apple's mobile devices lack a physical back button and don't display any system chrome actions for native apps.

But the presence of a "back" button in the header has unnecessarily migrated to mobile web experiences. Many devices (Android, Blackberry, Windows Phone 7, etc.) have physical back buttons (FIG 4.13). Even Apple's mobile web browser includes a prominent back control in the application toolbar (FIG 4.14). Adding another back button in your mobile

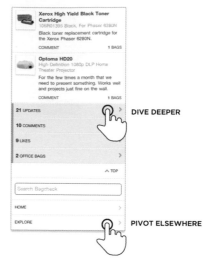

FIG 4.10: Contextual navigation menus on the Bagcheck mobile web experience allow people to explore related content.

DIVE DEEPER

PIVOT ELSEWHERE

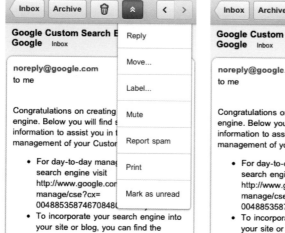

FIG 4.11: Contextual actions in the Gmail mobile web experience allow people to quickly act on their email.

FIG 4.12: The "back" button is a common feature in native iPhone applications.

Back Button

Back Button

FIG 4.13: Android devices feature a hardware back button on the device.

Back Button

Back Button

FIG 4.14: Apple's mobile web browser has a permanent back button in the bottom toolbar.

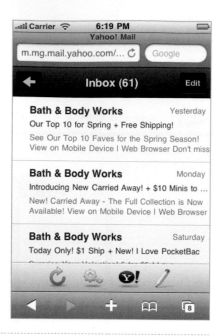

web experience's header only confuses things. Someone using the site must ask, "Do both of these back buttons do the same thing?"

So when designing mobile web experiences, you can leave "back" back in the native app. If you need to provide people with a quick way to go "up" a level in your site consider a label other than "back."

STICKING TO THE BOTTOM

Speaking of native iPhone applications, many of them also use fixed position navigation bars at the bottom of the screen. These menus make key actions easier to access with our thumbs, but unlike mobile web experiences, native iOS applications don't have web browser controls eating into their screen space. Yahoo! Mail's mobile web experience illustrates

FIG 4.16: Many devices have physical controls below the screen.

the impact browser chrome can have on a mobile web page. The two browser menus and two fixed position menus in Yahoo! Mail's mobile web experience leave little room for actually seeing what's in your inbox (FIG 4.15).

But mobile web experiences don't just have to contend with the chrome of one web browser on iOS: they have to contend with many web browsers. Devices with physical controls below their screen also present a challenge for menus fixed to the bottom of the screen (FIG 4.16). The close proximity of these controls and an application's menu bar means errors are bound to happen as people miss menus and hit physical buttons.

When developing a native mobile application you could adjust a menu's position to account for physical buttons below the screen, but mobile web experiences need to work across platforms—physical buttons below the screen or not.

So while navigation menus fixed to the bottom of the screen might be a good idea in some native mobile applications, the variable presence of web browser menus and physical controls below the screen on mobile devices means they are often a poor idea in mobile web experiences. If you need a fixed menu, better to fix it to the top, as Twitter has done in their redesigned mobile mobile web experience (FIG 4.17).

FIG 4.17: Twitter's latest mobile web experience uses a top navigation menu for key actions to account for the differences between mobile web devices.

MAINTAIN CLARITY AND FOCUS

As I mentioned in the first half of this book, when they are on their mobile devices, people are often just "one eyeball and one thumb." They're usually not comfortably seated in front of a desk and focused on your site. Instead, they are in the real world with many possible distractions around them. In these situations we only have people's partial attention; they need clear, focused designs to get things done—not lots of navigation options getting in their way.

Yahoo! Mail's compose email screen is a great example of removing extraneous actions and letting people focus on their primary task (in this case, writing an email) on their mobile device. This screen contains only a single navigation action: "cancel" (FIG 4.18). The rest of the interface is laser-focused on the task at hand.

ESPN's real-time updates of NBA games, on the other hand, are covered with so many navigation options that the display of what's happening in the game is pushed off screen. The

FIG 4.18: Contrast the amount of navigation options in Yahoo's Compose Mail (left) and ESPN's live game screens (right).

task at hand is seeing play-by-play action not jumping between menu options.

Minimizing the amount of navigation options on mobile screens helps to prevent errors as well. With fewer navigation choices, people are less likely to accidentally tap away to other tasks while trying to accomplish their current objective.

ORGANIZING MOBILE

When organizing your mobile web experience, think through how you can align mobile behaviors with your customer's needs.

- Mobile use cases like lookup/find, explore/play, check-in/status, and edit/create allow you to think through how your site will be used on mobile and adjust its structure appropriately.

- Focusing on content first, navigation second gets people to the information and tasks they want quickly.
- Relevant and well-placed navigation options allow people to dive deeper or pivot to explore other parts of your site.
- Reducing the amount of navigation choices and chrome on key tasks maintains clarity and focus on what people need to accomplish—helpful when they are hurried or in less than ideal situations.
- And when they do have some relaxing time on the couch with their mobile, people will still appreciate the simplicity of your design!

Getting your mobile web experience organized will help people find their way around; but once they find what they're looking for, they need to act on it. Next, let's look at how they can do just that.

5 ACTIONS

WHEN SCREENS ARE SMALL and used in our hands, touch screens make a lot of sense. They essentially turn the entire mobile device (not just the keypad or trackball) into an interactive surface. As a result, touch is being integrated into more and more mobile devices each day. Looking at the percentage of Nokia's smartphones that support touch illustrates this story very well (FIG 5.1).

While some of these devices have hardware input controls like trackpads, trackwheels, and keyboards, it's touch that increasingly manages people's interactions with the web on mobile. So how can we ensure everyone is able to interact with our sites using touch? Designing the right affordances and controls for touch-based user interfaces requires.

- Ensuring that touch targets are appropriately sized and positioned.
- Being familiar with common touch gestures and how they map to people's objectives.

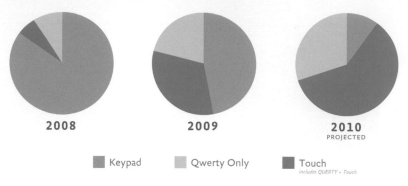

2008

2009

2010
PROJECTED

■ Keypad ■ Qwerty Only ■ Touch
includes QWERTY + Touch

FIG 5.1: Nokia's smartphones illustrate the transition to touch in mobile devices. (Source: Nokia.)

- Covering the loss of hover-based interactions.
- Making sure we don't forget about indirect manipulation along the way.

GO SMALL BY GOING BIG

It's not uncommon for web designers to respond to smaller mobile devices by shrinking things down in order to fit them on screen. After all, there's less room to work with, so smaller is better, right? Despite the soundness of this reasoning, you actually want to move in the opposite direction and make things bigger—often even bigger than you're naturally comfortable with (**FIG 5.2**).

Human fingers are imprecise pointing instruments: they lack the pixel-level accuracy of a mouse pointer; they come in different sizes; and it's not uncommon for them to slip or move around as we interact with our devices. Bigger actions mean bigger touch targets that help people get things done when they are in "one eyeball and one thumb" mode.

Just how bad is it? One study found that almost half of mobile app users are more likely to tap an ad by mistake than intentionally (http://bkaprt.com/mf/41). Appropriately sized

FIG 5.2: Actions on YouTube's mobile web experience are big enough to use with one thumb and few errors.

and placed actions (and thereby touch targets) can help people tap with confidence and accuracy. So just how big is just right?

In their iOS Human Interface Guidelines (http://bkaprt.com/mf/42), Apple recommends making touch targets 44×44 points. They use points instead of pixels to deal with differences in screen density, which we'll discuss in more depth later on. To account for screen density (or ppi) variations, it's better to measure touch targets in physical dimensions.

Microsoft takes this approach in their Windows Phone 7 Guidelines by recommending 9mm touch targets, a minimum size of 7mm, and a minimum spacing between actions of 2mm. Other touch-UI guidelines from Nokia (and even Ubuntu) fall in the same range because they all take the average size of people's fingers into account. MIT's Touch Lab determined that average to be 10–14mm for finger pads and 8–10mm for fingertips (http://bkaprt.com/mf/43).

Taking these touch-target sizing recommendations into account doesn't necessarily mean every icon and button on your mobile page needs to be exactly 9mm wide and 9mm tall. The

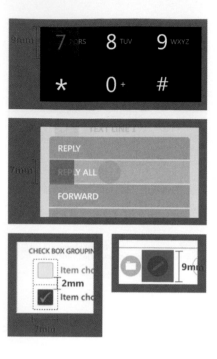

FIG 5.3: Microsoft's Windows Phone 7 Touch target guidelines.

touch target itself should fall in this range, but the visual representation of the action can be 50-100% of the actual touch target size. The image from Microsoft (**FIG 5.3**) illustrates the use of padding or margins to ensure targets are the right size without having every visible user interface element appear the same.

Microsoft's guidelines also do a nice job of specifying when touch targets may need to be bigger than 9mm: if "the UI element is frequently touched; the result of a touch error is severe or really frustrating; the UI element is located toward the edge of the screen or difficult to hit; or when the UI element is part of a sequential task—like using the dial pad," (http://bkaprt.com/mf/44; PDF).

When it comes to what we touch on mobile, bigger is generally better. Ensuring actions are appropriately sized and spaced apart can avoid serious usability issues as well—not

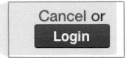

FIG 5.4: Quora's login screen places "Cancel" and "Login" much too close for touch-target comfort.

just accidental slips of the finger. Take a close look at the mobile login screen of Q&A site Quora (FIG 5.4). Notice any potential problems?

That's right, in this case poorly sized and spaced actions (remember 2mm between touch targets!) mean the difference between logging in and canceling out.

Flickr's advanced search screen is another example of being too close to touch comfortably (FIG 5.5). The size and spacing between each search option could definitely benefit from "bigger is better."

WHERE DO WE TOUCH?

When talking about the placement of navigation controls earlier, I mentioned that actions toward the bottom of the device naturally align with how people hold and use their mobiles. Well, there's a bit more to it than that. Where you expect to find primary actions on a touch-screen mobile often depends

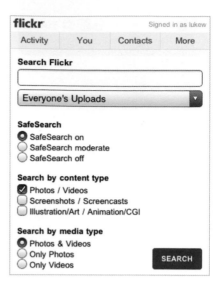

FIG 5.5: Flickr's Advanced Search options are too close together and too small to tap accurately.

on which fingers (thumb or index) you are using for tapping and if you are right or left-handed.

Since the majority of people are right-handed (about 70-90%) and use their thumbs while operating a mobile with one hand, optimizing for right-thumb actions is most common. This means primary actions can be placed in the middle or bottom of the screen and arranged from left to right (**FIG 5.6**).

Destructive actions like cancel or delete can be placed outside people's comfort zone. If you're holding a mobile device in your right hand and using your thumb to operate it, getting to the upper left corner is a stretch. It's uncomfortable and you have to work for it. It's perfect for making you think twice about deleting all the hard work you just did.

LEARN THE LANGUAGE OF TOUCH

While touch targets can ensure we have appropriately sized actions on our mobile web experiences, touch gestures give people a way to interact with them. Despite different terms and documentation for touch gestures in the various mobile

FIG 5.6: While holding a touch screen phone with only your right hand, it's easy to hit the dark green area and a stretch to tap the yellow area with your thumb.

platforms out there today, there's a good deal of consistency in the gestures we can expect people to use on our mobile web experiences.

To better understand what's available, Dan Willis, Craig Villamor, and I combed through the documentation for:

- Apple's iOS and OS X,
- Google's Android,
- Microsoft's Windows Phone 7, Windows 7, and Surface,
- Palm's WebOS,
- GestureWorks' Flash support,
- And even Wacom's Bamboo touch-enabled drawing tablet.

Thankfully in our audit we found more consistency than diversity. In fact, there's a set of core touch gestures that are

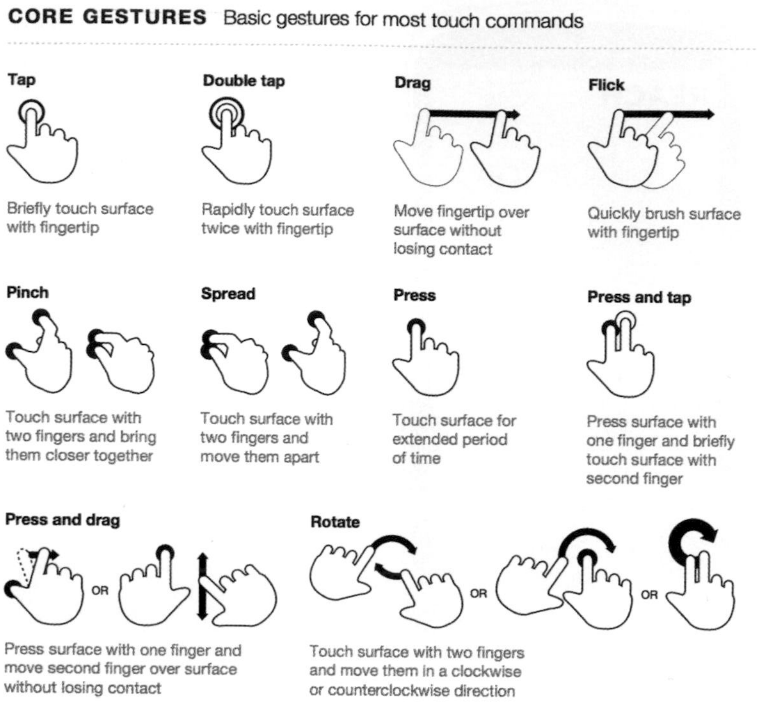

CORE GESTURES Basic gestures for most touch commands

Tap

Briefly touch surface
with fingertip

Double tap

Rapidly touch surface
twice with fingertip

Drag

Move fingertip over
surface without
losing contact

Flick

Quickly brush surface
with fingertip

Pinch

Touch surface with
two fingers and bring
them closer together

Spread

Touch surface with
two fingers and
move them apart

Press

Touch surface for
extended period
of time

Press and tap

Press surface with
one finger and briefly
touch surface with
second finger

Press and drag

OR

Press surface with one finger and
move second finger over surface
without losing contact

Rotate

OR   OR

Touch surface with two fingers
and move them in a clockwise
or counterclockwise direction

FIG 5.7: Core touch gestures: basic gestures for most touch commands.

common across most touch platforms. These gestures form
the basis of how you can expect people to interact with touch
screens; they include: tap, double tap, drag, swipe, pinch,
spread, press, press and tap, press and drag, and several variations on rotate. And because of spotty multi-touch support
and "reserved" system actions in some mobile web browsers,
this list can be even further reduced for mobile web experiences to tap, drag, and swipe (FIG 5.7).

While it's useful to know what touch gestures are possible,
it's even better to have a sense of how people are using these
gestures to interact with touch-based user interfaces. In other
words, if someone wants to take action on an object or screen,

or to navigate between objects and screens, which touch gestures are they mostly likely to use? The Touch Gesture Reference Guide created from our initial audit answers these questions and more (http://bkaprt.com/mf/45) (**FIG 5.8**).

You can get a sense of how the guide is organized in these examples. It starts with what someone hopes to accomplish, such as changing modes, deleting an object, or scrolling a list. Next to each of these potential actions are the most commonly supported (and increasingly expected) gestures used to get it done.

The Touch Gesture Reference Guide is freely available and includes templates for every core gesture in PDF, EPS, OmniGraffle, and Visio so you can use them in your wireframes, mock-ups, and prototypes as well. So have at it!

Widespread adoption of touch UIs is really just happening now, which means we can expect to see new touch-based design solutions continue to emerge. Gesture-based actions like "pull down to refresh" often start out in a single application, slowly become adopted in more places, and over time become expected by the people using your sites. So don't be afraid to experiment with what gestures can do (**FIG 5.9-5.10**).

DON'T FEAR THE NUI

I, for one, welcome our NUI overloads. That is, I believe in the potential of natural user interfaces (NUIs) to push us toward a new era of computing. NUI principles—such as make content the user interface; enable direct interactions with content not chrome; and reduce visuals that are not content—drive us toward a more direct way of interacting with digital information and media.

Gone are the days when you need to make use of windows, icons, menus, and pointers (WIMP) to zoom into a photo. Simply touch the photo and spread you fingers apart to make it bigger. This direct interaction is not only easier to learn (just ask all the kids and grandparents on iPads) but more reflective of how we actually interact with the real world as well.

As great as that sounds, we're still in a transition period between graphical user interfaces (GUIs) and NUIs. As a result,

BASIC ACTIONS		
user action	gesture	description
Change mode	 press	Touch surface for extended period of time
Select	 tap	Briefly touch surface with fingertip

OBJECT-RELATED ACTIONS		
user action	gesture	description
Delete	 drag (across item or off-screen)	Move fingertip over surface without losing contact
Duplicate	 tap (source and destination)	Touch object, then touch elsewhere on surface

NAVIGATING ACTIONS		
user action	gesture	description
Scroll	 drag	Move fingertip over scrollbar without losing contact
Scroll (fast)	 flick	Quickly brush surface with fingertip in the direction you want to scroll

FIG 5.8: A sample of user actions and the gestures that support them.

actions that rely solely on gestures might not be immediately discoverable by everyone using our web experiences. So for now, we may need to stick with buttons for the primary actions in our mobile web experiences. But that's no reason not to experiment with gestures in other parts of our sites, like advanced controls or shortcuts.

FIG 5.9: Yahoo! Mail's mobile web experience allows people to use touch gestures to reveal mail actions and pull down to expose search. Because there are no visible affordances for these gestures, they introduce people to them in an overview up front.

FIG 5.10: Twitter's mobile web experience allows people to use the drag (down) gesture to refresh the screen.

When you do, try to align with natural gestures (those common to us in our daily lives) in order to aid discovery. A recent study across nine different countries found very few cultural differences in the gestures people attempted to use for

FEB 9, 2011 UPDATED 11:19PM ET

FINAL		FINAL		F/OT	
▶ DET	103	CHA	103	NOR	101
CLE	94	▶ IND	104	▶ NJN	103

FIG 5.11: ESPN's mobile web experience uses a visual affordance common to swipe gestures, but this particular menu can't actually be swiped.

common tasks (http://bkaprt.com/mf/46). So when it comes to touch, we have a lot in common.

Lastly, visible affordances, tips, and animations can help ease the transition as well. You can start out by using these interface elements to explicitly call out where gestures are possible, then gradually reduce their presence as people become more familiar with where they can use gestures to get things done. Just be aware that when you've got too much help text explaining how things work, the gesture-based interactions in your app might not be as natural as you think.

Also make sure you set the right expectations about gestures. Though the NBA scoreboard on ESPN's mobile web experience above looks like it can be swiped, you actually have to use the arrows to move between scores (**FIG 5.11**).

COVER THE HOVER

Since we're on the topic of tips, it's worth noting that any tips or actions that happen "on hover" (when a mouse pointer is positioned over a trigger) won't work the same way on touch-only devices. Quite simply, there is no pointer to position over an interface element. There's just our fingers, and though they cast a shadow, no mobile device I know of considers that a hover yet.

Therefore, any actions that rely on mouse hovers in our desktop web experiences need to be rethought—and that's a good thing. Many uses of hover actions on the web assume too much. Just because someone places their mouse cursor over something doesn't mean they are asking for a pop-up

FIG 5.12: Placing your mouse cursor over a book's title on Barnes & Noble's website brings up a pop-up window with just a bit more info.

menu of actions and options (**FIG 5.12**). Unlike clicks, hovers are usually not explicit actions.

On-hover menus on the web have also become dumping grounds for actions not deemed important enough to be on the screen but still important enough to reveal on hover. Often that amounts to a miscellaneous bin of options that really don't have a place as primary controls on a screen. These hovers won't be missed when you make the transition to mobile.

On mobile, your options for on-hover menus are: on screen, on tap/swipe, on a separate screen, or (my favorite) gone for good.

On screen

If what's in a hover is important enough, taking actions and information out of on-hover menus and placing them directly on the screen could be the right approach. This is the solution Twitter used on their original mobile web experience.

On the desktop, placing your mouse over a message on Twitter reveals several important actions: Favorite, Retweet, and Reply (**FIG 5.13**).

Twitter thought these actions were important enough that in their mobile web experience, they placed them directly on the screen (**FIG 5.14**).

kentbrew Kent Brewster
Laid-back night tonight; high point was dinner on the sidewalk with
@chaddickerson and the @etsy crew.
4 minutes ago

kentbrew Kent Brewster
Laid-back night tonight; high point was dinner on the sidewalk with
@chaddickerson and the @etsy crew.
4 minutes ago ☆ Favorite ↻ Retweet ↩ Reply

FIG 5.13: Hovering over an update on Twitter reveals a few additional actions.

FIG 5.14: Twitter's original mobile web experience made Favorite, Retweet, and Reply visible at all times.

On tap or swipe

Depending on the mobile web browser, if you do nothing with the hover menus on your existing website, they could be turned into on-tap menus by default. This might be good if the actions or content in the hover menu are a logical next step for people. But it could be annoying if the hover menu

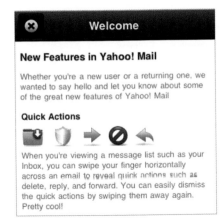

content introduces an unneeded extra step that gets in the way of people's progress.

Swipe gestures are less discoverable than tap and likely require some extra development work to get right, but they won't get in people's way like on-tap actions that aren't part of a logical sequence. If you do use swipe gestures, you may want to include an affordance—or light animation—to let people know how things work (**FIG 5.15**).

It's also important to note that actions and information revealed using a non-obvious touch gesture (like a swipe), should have some alternate way of being accessed. In Yahoo! Mail, the actions revealed on swipe are also included on the full email screen (**FIG 5.16**).

On a separate screen

If the content within a hover is extensive, it may be best to move what's inside the hover menu to a separate screen on mobile. This is the approach used by Barnes & Noble (**FIG 5.17**). What used to be a large (and annoying) hover menu on their desktop site is now a separate page on their mobile web experience.

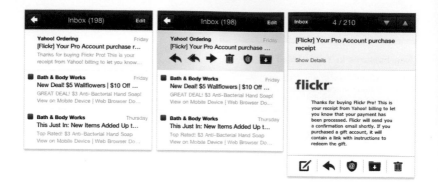

FIG 5.16: Yahoo! Mail's touch gesture shortcuts are also present on the message screen.

Gone for good

If there was never any value in your hover menus to begin with, just get rid of what's inside them entirely. Removing extra options and information that's not valuable to your customers not only simplifies your product's user interface, it also gives you less to develop and maintain over time. So don't be afraid to toss those hover menus out.

Whichever approach is right for you, just make sure when you go mobile your hovers have been covered.

CAN'T TOUCH THIS

Just when you thought we were done: covering hovers also includes thinking about and designing for non-touch and hybrid devices as well. Mobiles with indirect manipulation modes for input—such as trackpads, trackballs, keypads, scrollwheels, and physical keyboards—allow you to use the web without getting your fingers all over the screen.

When people navigate a web page using these types of intermediary controls, the CSS :hover state can be used to highlight the currently focused interface element without using JavaScript. While it may be better to set a style for this

FIG 5.17: The content in the hover menu on the desktop is a separate screen on the mobile website.

mode using the :focus state, many websites don't specify an implicit :focus state. So mobile browsers like OperaMini, do the best they can and use :hover to let people know which element is currently actionable from those visible on screen.

All the actionable links, buttons, and menus on your mobile web experience can benefit from having explicitly defined :hover and :focus states. This will provide valuable feedback to anyone using your site or application through indirect manipulation hardware on a mobile device.

But when thinking about non-touch mobile devices, we don't just have to worry about focus. While most of the big smartphone manufacturers have fully embraced touch, not all the devices they released in the past and will continue to ship in the future have touch screens. On these devices, appropriately sized touch targets will take up too much room (as non-touch mobile devices often have smaller screens), and touch gestures will be non-existent. So we need to adapt.

The layout techniques we will discuss later in the book can help your sites adjust to make interactive targets smaller, while thoughtful uses of progressive enhancement can ensure basic interactive actions still work. But I promised not to get into development and to keep this book short, so I'll save the overview of progressive enhancement to people more qualified than me (http://bkaprt.com/mf/47).

READY, SET, ACTIONS

As more touch-screen mobile devices get into people's hands, we need to make sure they can use our websites with their hands. To do so:

- Go big with appropriately sized and positioned touch targets.
- Learn the language of touch by familiarizing yourself with common touch gestures and how they are used to navigate and interact with objects and screens.
- Don't be afraid to push toward natural user interfaces (NUIs) that make content (not chrome) the focus of people's actions.
- Transition your on-hover menus to mobile using the most appropriate solution for your site.
- Remember to consider non-touch and hybrid devices when designing your mobile web interactions.

Now that we've covered the basics of actions, let's turn our attention to the most important action of all: input.

6 INPUTS

THE POWER OF THE WEB has always come from people's ability to not only view and consume content, but to contribute and create content as well. Input on mobile is just as important as output, but like all things mobile it typically requires its own bit of secret sauce:

- Embrace mobile as an opportunity for people to contribute and create whenever and wherever inspiration strikes.
- Use mobile-optimized labels to clearly ask questions.
- Take advantage of input types, attributes, and masks to make mobile input easier.
- Choose the right layouts for sequential, non-linear, and in-context forms.
- Look for opportunities to go beyond the input field using mobile device capabilities.

EMBRACING INPUT

Designers don't always agree. So it's somewhat surprising to look back at mobile design guidelines from the past few years and see a lot of consensus around input. At the time, pretty much everyone concurred that most kinds of mobile input should be avoided. In *Mobile Web Design and Development* (O'Reilly, 2009), Brian Fling wrote: "The rule of thumb is to limit the use of forms in the mobile context."

But while there are lots of great reasons to avoid requiring precise input when people are just "one eyeball and one thumb," there are just as many reasons to let people contribute as much as they see fit from their mobile devices. After all, over four billion text messages were sent per day in the United States in 2010—many of them through painful feature phone keypads. Clearly people want to message each other using their mobiles—a lot. And they are willing to endure hardship to do it.

But things don't have to be so hard. Modern mobile devices are continuing to make it easier to provide input through larger touch screens, microphones, video cameras, and more. So it's high time we stop thinking of input as something to avoid and instead think of mobile as an incredible opportunity for getting lots of diverse input from people.

Mobile devices are with us all the time. So whenever or wherever inspiration strikes we can speak our mind, share, or just contribute online. Capabilities like location detection, device orientation, audio, video cameras, and more, give us new ways to provide input that don't require lots of typing with imprecise fingers.

Most importantly, though, we need to stop assuming that people won't do things just because they are on their mobile devices. After all, someone bought a $265,000 plane using eBay's iPhone app (http://bkaprt.com/mf/48, http://bkaprt.com/mf/49)! Once we come to terms with the fact that mobile input should be welcomed and encouraged, we can start talking about how to design for it.

MOBILE ASKS

How we ask people for their input goes a long way toward determining the kind of answers we'll get. On the web, most questions are asked through forms, and forms use labels to ask for what they need. Form labels on mobile, however, come with their own set of constraints and capabilities that determine how they should be designed.

Screens on mobile are small and web forms need to adjust. In most cases, there isn't room for left-aligned or right-aligned labels because there isn't enough room for two columns on a mobile device's display. Instead, top-aligned labels work best; not only do they optimize for screen real estate and accommodate longer labels easily, they also stay visible when a virtual keyboard is present and taking up half of the room available on screen.

Twitter's mobile sign-up form (**FIG 6.1**) uses top aligned labels to ask questions and includes supporting text below the input field for clarification and additional details. Both of these elements remain visible when a virtual keyboard is present. And while we're on the subject of Twitter, did you know that 16% of new Twitter users in a five-month period during 2010 signed up through mobile (http://bkaprt.com/mf/25)? And 40% of all tweets come from a mobile device (http://bkaprt.com/mf/50)? Still don't think input on mobile matters?

Though top-aligned labels work well within the tight constraints of mobile screens, labels inside input fields can work even better. As proof, just about every native mobile application platform supports labels within input fields and uses them in their default applications. On the web, however, implementing labels within fields requires some work.

Though labels within input fields seem great on the surface, there are some challenges to overcome. A label within an input field:

- Should never become part of someone's answer. This seems simple enough but still happens quite frequently when things haven't been loaded or aren't coded correctly.

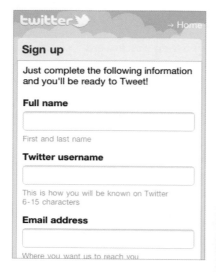

FIG 6.1: Twitter's mobile sign-up form makes good use of top-aligned labels.

Ever try searching only to find the word "search" has become part of your query?

- Should not be confused with an actual answer in an input field. If labels and inputs look too similar, people might (rightly) assume an answer has already been provided for them. I've seen this happen too often in usability testing.
- Is usually absent when someone starts answering a question and when they finish answering a set of questions. This can make it harder to know which question is being answered or to go back and check answers after the labels are gone.

The mobile sign-in screen for email-marketing site MailChimp highlights two of these points (FIG 6.2). When entering a username into the first input field, the label inside disappears. (Note: this is default behavior for the HTML5

FIG 6.2: MailChimp's mobile sign-in form illustrates some of the challenges with labels inside input fields.

input attribute `placeholder` which, according to the spec, is intended for tips, not labels.) After an answer has been provided, the difference in color between the answer ("lukew") and the next label ("password") is just a subtle shade of gray. Neither of these two issues are likely to be a very big problem in such a simple form. But as forms get longer, problems stemming from these issues can get a lot worse.

There are, however, ways to mitigate things so that labels within input fields work better. The mobile sign-in screen for the project management application Basecamp keeps labels within input fields visible until someone actually begins to enter an answer. (This requires some development work as it currently isn't default web browser behavior.) Basecamp also makes a stronger visual distinction between answers and labels so the two are less likely to be confused (**FIG 6.3**).

MOBILE ANSWERS

Truthfully, asking questions on mobile with well-designed labels isn't the hard part. Making it as easy as possible for people to answer accurately is. Thankfully, mobile isn't just full of constraints; there are also a lot of capabilities that can help us out as well.

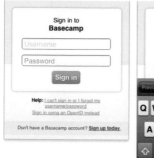

FIG 6.3: 37signal's Basecamp has put in some extra work to make labels within input fields better in their sign-in form.

The standards

If you've been working on the web for a while, you're probably familiar with input types. The most commonly used and widely supported input types are checkbox, radio, password, select menus (dropdown lists), file pick, submit buttons, and plain text. Sticking to these standards, where appropriate, can do a lot to help people on mobile (TABLE 6.1).

For example, when you use a standard select menu for a dropdown list, a mobile touch-screen browser may provide a large swipe-able list with appropriately sized touch targets, rather than the standard dropdown menus found on the desktop (FIG 6.4–6.5). Different mobile platforms will manage these lists differently, but all of them try to make it easier to provide input when using standard controls. The same applies to submit buttons, radio buttons, error messages, and more.

Beyond the standards

But there are exceptions. Though mobile platform controls for select menus usually make it easier for people to pick an answer from a list, they sometimes get stretched to their limits. If the contents of a select menu run long, they can be cut off

INPUT TYPE	HTML
checkbox	`<input type="checkbox">`
radio button	`<input type="radio">`
password field	`<input type="password">`
dropdown lists	`<select><option>...`
file picker	`<input type="file">`
submit button	`<input type="submit">`
plain text	`<input type="text">`

TABLE 6.1: Standard input types on the web

when displayed at a larger "zoomed" size making it hard for people to read through their options (**FIG 6.6**).

When displayed within a custom control, lengthy select menus also don't get the full screen height available. Instead, people are forced to find the option they are looking for by scrolling within a smaller window. On a device like the iPhone, you can only see four to five options at once.

So if the content within one of your select menus is going to stretch the vertical or horizontal limits of a standard select control, you're probably better off with a separate page on mobile that allows people to pick the option they need from a full-screen list.

You may also opt to leave select menus behind when a simple touch control can get the job done faster and easier. As it turns out, select menus are pretty tap-intensive: tap the menu once to open it, swipe the list that shows up to find the answer you want to select, tap it, and then tap done or close to go back to the form. That's four taps (just in case you weren't counting). So it's not hard to see that when a form uses several select menus (**FIG 6.7**), the taps can quickly add up.

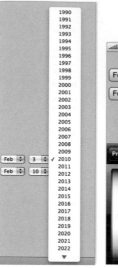

FIG 6.4: The iPhone's mobile browser uses a touch-optimized (swipe-able, big touch targets) control for standard select menus.

FIG 6.5: Android's mobile web browser also optimizes select menus for touch.

Luckily, we can be a lot more tap-efficient with a few custom controls designed specifically for touch-based interfaces. Instead of using select menus to set the number of guests and rooms, the travel site Kayak (**FIG 6.8**) uses a spinner control. This input only requires a single tap to adjust (just hit the "+" or "-") and works well for questions that have a small range of

FIG 6.6: The list of possible questions on Microsoft's signup form stretches an iOS select menu's control to the limit.

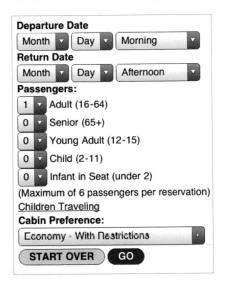

FIG 6.7: Booking a flight on American Airlines' mobile web experience is a select-menu full affair.

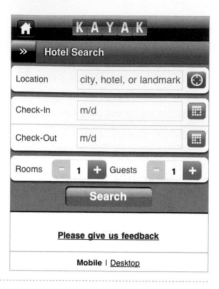

FIG 6.8: Kayak uses a touch-optimized spinner control for selecting rooms or guests in their hotel booking form.

options. For example, you can only book up to two hotel rooms on Kayak.

The rooms and guests fields in Kayak's form also make things easier for people on mobile by starting them off with smart defaults—selections put in place that serve the interests of most people (http://bkaprt.com/mf/51). When booking a hotel, the majority of Kayak's customers only need one room. Setting this value to "1" instead of asking people to enter it themselves saves time and effort.

In fact, a study comparing empty forms on mobile to pre-filled forms that only required adjusting a few default values, found people were four times faster with smart defaults than empty fields (http://bkaprt.com/mf/52; PDF). On mobile those kinds of savings go a long way.

Kayak also uses a custom control for their date picker. Instead of the three select menus American Airlines used for date selection (FIG 6.7), the date picker on Kayak's mobile web experience uses appropriately sized touch targets that allow people to tap between months and select the days they want to travel (FIG 6.9). Once again, saving people from a bunch of unnecessary tapping around.

FIG 6.9: Kayak's date picker makes use of appropriately sized touch targets.

If you decide to use custom input controls in your mobile web experience to make things more efficient on touch screens, don't forget about non-touch and hybrid devices. Make sure your controls can be used through indirect manipulation (trackballs, trackpads, etc.) by specifying a tab order within the web form and setting :focus and :hover states.

The new standards

In order to implement custom input controls we need to write custom code. But mobile web browsers are evolving extremely fast and elements that currently require a procedural solution may soon only need to be declared in markup (http://bkaprt.com/mf/53). In fact, there are a number of declarative solutions that can make input easier on mobile today.

For starters, several new HTML5 input types can help people accurately answer questions that require a specific format. On a mobile browser like Safari, specifying an input of type url brings up a virtual alphanumeric keyboard with ".", "/", and ".com" keys. Specifying an input of type email brings up

url

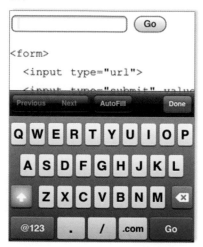

email

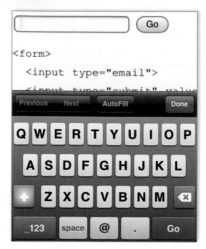

number

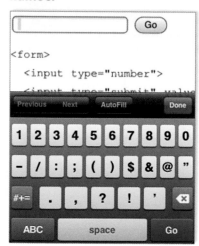

FIG 6.10: Using HTML5 input types and the specific virtual keyboards associated with them. Images from *Dive into HTML5* by Mark Pilgrim (http://bkaprt.com/mf/54).

a virtual alphanumeric keyboard with "." and "@" keys. And specifying an input of type number brings up a virtual numeric keyboard (**FIG 6.10**).

These input-specific keyboards make it easier to enter the exact type of data required by each input field. Older browsers that don't support new input types simply treat these fields as standard text inputs so there's little harm in using these HTML5 input types now. (You can see the input types supported by popular mobile web browsers in Peter-Paul Koch's compatibility table at http://bkaprt.com/mf/55.)

Even browsers without virtual keyboards benefit from specifying number input types (using HTML5 or lesser known standards like CSS-MP, or wireless CSS), because people do not have to switch to number mode to enter numeric data. And speaking of numbers, phones were actually designed for numerical input: virtual or not, most of them still have keypads. So when asking for numerical inputs like phone numbers or prices, use a single input field and allow people to rely on the keypad to provide an accurate answer.

Despite the introduction of new input types, a lot of the work in forms still falls on the plain text input. Luckily even plain text inputs on mobile can be made easier through the use of input attributes, including:

- *autocapitalize:* Turn this off on email, password, URL, and other case-sensitive fields; turn it on for proper nouns like names and locations.
- *autocorrect:* Turn this off on email, password, URL, and other non-alphabetical inputs; turn it on for text areas and free-form inputs; trim trailing spaces in inputs that might come from auto-correction features.

Once again, browsers that don't support these attributes will simply ignore them so there is no harm in including them in your designs. Where they do work, however, people will thank you after the answer they tap isn't eradicated by an over-zealous auto-correcting OS.

Email address

example@me.com

Email address

@me.com

Email address

luke@me.com

MASKING THE HARD STUFF

Specifying input types and attributes can help people on mobile provide accurate answers without a lot of work. But we can do even better by taking advantage of input masks. Input masks can help make complex inputs manageable on mobile by providing clear input cues up front and restricting people's inputs so they don't make mistakes.

Most mobile operating systems have built in support for input masks so it's not uncommon to find them inside native mobile applications. In the browser, however, a lot of the heavy lifting required to make input masks possible falls on us and JavaScript. As a result, it's useful to know what makes a good input mask work.

In its most basic form an input mask can ensure that an answer is entered in a valid format. To illustrate, let's imagine we need someone to provide his or her email address at me.com. We can use an input mask to "mask" or cover over anything that isn't part of the format we require. In this case, the email address we collect has to end in "@me.com" so we can mask any characters that are entered after the "@" to make sure a me.com email address is provided.

You can see this in action in **FIG 6.11**. As someone begins to enter an email address, the "@me.com" portion of the input remains visible. If any characters are entered after the "@" they are ignored. This not only cuts down on errors, it also

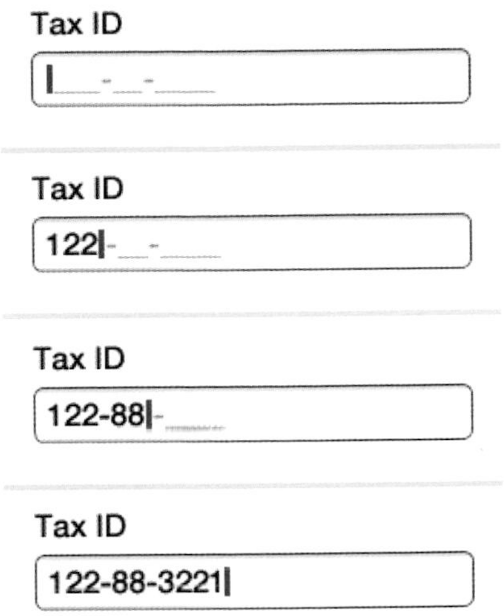

Tax ID

| I   -   - |

FIG 6.12: A well-designed input mask for entering a tax ID number.

Tax ID

| 122-   - |

Tax ID

| 122-88- |

Tax ID

| 122-88-3221 |

reduces the amount of input people need to provide, both of which are big benefits on mobile.

But there are a few design considerations we need to take into account in order to make sure input masks help (not hinder) people's ability to provide answers. First, it's a good idea to reveal the format an input requires up front. In the me.com example, the "@me.com" portion of the input was visible right away and stayed visible as someone entered his or her email address.

In the tax ID example (FIG 6.12), the structure of the number required is revealed right away and it stays visible as someone enters the answer. The input mask in this example will not only ignore any dashes (since they are already part of the formatting) but any non-numerical characters as well. So if you try entering an A or G, nothing happens. Since the tax ID required consists only of numbers and two dashes, this input mask prevents you from making a mistake by accidentally entering a letter.

But input masks can feel unpredictable (and thereby confusing) when they don't consistently communicate their expectations. In the phone number input mask example (FIG

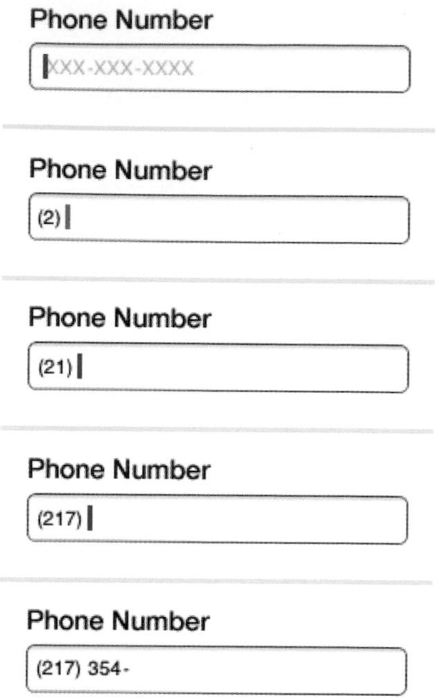

Phone Number

XXX-XXX-XXXX

Phone Number

(2)

Phone Number

(21)

Phone Number

(217)

Phone Number

(217) 354-

FIG 6.13: Don't gradually reveal input masks while people are trying to answer your question.

6.13), there's an expectation set that the number needs to be formatted as "XXX-XX-XXXX." (Note: I'd suggest "___-___-____" as it feels more like a question than an answer.) But as soon as you enter the first number, this format disappears, and two parentheses surround your input. That's unexpected. As you continue , the formatting required by this input field gradually reveals itself as numbers are entered.

When you're done, the final answer uses parentheses, a space, and one dash—not at all what was promised up front. For a commonly understood question like a phone number, this might not be a big deal. But as a general rule, input masks that stick to the expectations they set up front are easier to manage than ones that decide to gradually reveal themselves or show up after the fact. And we want input masks to make things easier on mobile, not more confusing.

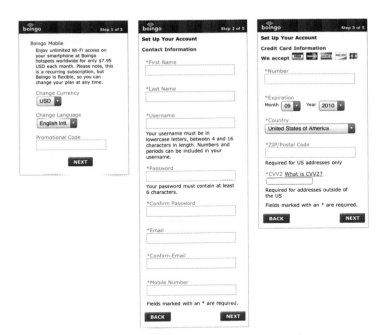

FIG 6.14: The original Boingo "Get Online" form had five separate screens. Here are just three of them.

LAYING OUT THE OPTIONS

While labels and input fields are the building blocks of forms, they ultimately need to come together as a conversation between organizations and their customers. In other words, we need to layout the input we're asking for appropriately. At a high-level, there are three input scenarios we have to consider: a sequence of related questions, non-linear updates, and in-context inputs for immediate responses.

A sequential set of inputs is a group of questions that have to be asked together in order to complete a task. The most common examples online are registration and checkout forms. But anything that requires people to provide answers to a set of questions before they can accomplish their goal (of

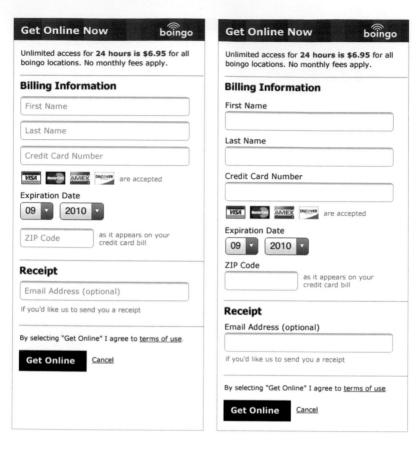

FIG 6.15: My quick redesign of the Boingo form cut things down to a single screen that lets people get online fast.

signing up, buying something, etc.) counts as a sequential set of inputs.

While the label and input field best practices we discussed in this chapter can go a long way toward making sequential forms easier to complete on mobile, the quantity of information you require people to fill out is likely to have the most direct impact. The fewer questions you ask, the better. Compare the original Boingo "Get Online" form (**FIG 6.14**)

FIG 6.16: Editing your profile on Bagcheck uses a dialog window for each input.

with my redesign (FIG 6.15) to see just how much can be cut when you aim to be concise. When it comes to mobile forms, be brutally efficient and trim, trim, trim.

But we don't always need people to answer a bunch of our questions at once. There are many situations where only some inputs (in a bigger set) need to be updated or adjusted. In these situations, exposing input fields for every possible answer makes it hard to find the one or two inputs you need to adjust—especially on small mobile screens.

So for non-linear input updates a different kind of layout makes sense. For example, editing your profile information on Bagcheck is a rare occurrence and editing every part of your profile is rarer still. As a result, the "Edit Profile" screen lists available inputs and their current answers but doesn't expose all the input fields for these answers by default. Instead, each possible input can be tapped and edited in a dialog window (to set focus and pop-up the virtual keyboard immediately) or on a separate screen (FIG 6.16).

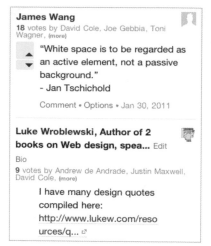

FIG 6.17: An in-context comment form on Quora's mobile web experience.

When designing single input screen or dialogs, make sure you take the height of virtual keyboards into account (usually half the screen height). It's best if the input and actions are visible while the keyboard is present so people can see their answers and options.

Last but not least, in-context inputs provide a way for people to quickly contribute or create without a lot of effort. An in-context input shows up directly inline where people can contribute and usually only consists of a single input field. For example, Quora allows you to comment directly on an answer without leaving the current screen (FIG 6.17); this enables immediate contributions and aligns well with the quick ways people often use their mobile devices.

BEYOND FORMS AND INPUT FIELDS

Today's mobile devices are full of capabilities that take us beyond the input field. Location detection, device orientation, audio input, video input, near field communications, and

FIG 6.18: One tap access to your current location on Kayak and Twitter means no typing is required.

more can be used to allow people to participate and contribute without typing into a form.

To illustrate, let's look at location detection. When booking a hotel on Kayak, you can enter a location using the keyboard, or you can use your current location by tapping the icon to the right of the input field. Similarly, Twitter allows you to append a location to your post with a single tap (FIG 6.18). No typing required.

On the other side of the spectrum, Google Goggles uses the video camera on a mobile device to identify products, wines, works of art, and landmarks; to scan in business cards; or to translate foreign languages (FIG 6.19). Imagine all the typing you'd have to do in a form to accomplish what Google Goggles does when you simply point your camera at something.

And near field communications (NFC) can take this even further. Mobile devices that can communicate with radio frequency ID tags (RFID) just need to be near something that broadcasts its identity using one of these tiny "digital bar-codes" in order to interact with it. Want to learn more about a

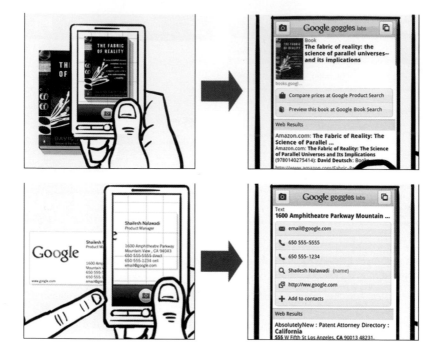

FIG 6.19: Google Goggles allows you to use the video camera on a mobile device for input.

product? Just get close enough for it to catch a signal and your mobile can bring up all the information you need. How's that for going beyond input fields and forms?

Once again though, I need to ground us in the current realities of the web. Native mobile applications have access to device APIs that let them access audio, video, NFC (where possible) and more. While there are many standards being written and debated for camera and NFC access in the web browser, widely available support is not here yet. But if the past is any indicator, new capabilities are probably making their way into mobile web browsers as this book is being printed. So don't fret; soon device APIs will be yours to use as well.

INPUT A GO-GO

Though people have clung to their mobile devices for years, opportunities for input on these devices have largely been ignored. But today's combination of more capable devices, better networks, and people's increasing desire to share make mobile input an opportunity you can't ignore.

- Actively encourage input and allow people to contribute and create using their mobile devices.
- Make sure your questions are clearly presented with mobile-optimized labels.
- Get rid of the pain associated with accurate mobile inputs by using input types, attributes, and masks in your designs where possible.
- Consider using custom input controls if they really help people provide accurate answers without a lot of work.
- Lay input possibilities out appropriately for sequential, non-linear, and in-context contributions.
- Take advantage of mobile device capabilities to capture input in new ways.

Now that we've tackled inputs, actions, and organization on mobile, we need to address the variety of devices where all these elements will live. Which brings us to our next chapter: layout.

LAYOUT

APPROPRIATE ADAPTATIONS of how we think about organization, actions, and input on the desktop take what we know about web design and make it usable on mobile. But how do we ensure it's also usable across the wide range of mobile devices available now and in the coming months—not to mention years?

- Come to terms with the fact that mobile is going to change at a breakneck pace for the foreseeable future.
- Let mobile browsers know you are creating designs that fit them.
- Be flexible, fluid, and responsive in your layouts.
- Know where to sketch the lines between device experiences.
- Reduce to the minimum amount necessary.

THE ONLY CONSTANT IS CHANGE

During the time I've been thinking about and writing this book, the mobile industry has changed dramatically several times. Mobile platform leaders have been unseated. Devices with new capabilities and constraints have been released. New partnerships between device manufacturers, mobile platform vendors, and network carriers have been announced.

Welcome to mobile where the only thing you can count on is change. Because things are currently in a continuous state of flux, I've focused this book on design principles for mobile device trends that have been holding steady for quite a while: more powerful processors, faster networks, touch-screen interfaces, and better web browsers. Despite my best attempts to give you mobile design principles that will endure, change is coming.

So what's a web designer to do—get swept up in a sea of constant instability? Quite the opposite. Because things continue to be so Wild West out there, you need to be a cowboy. Take risks, try new things, and accept that not all the boundary lines between devices, browsers, and the web have been drawn yet.

With that in mind, let's saddle up and talk about how to round up the diversity of devices out there with mobile layout skills. (And I promise that's it for the Old West analogy.)

YOU'RE HERE FOR THEM

Perhaps the most important thing we can do to create effective mobile layouts is to let mobile web browsers know we've taken the time to design for them. While I promised not to get into code, knowing about the meta viewport tag is really useful for designing mobile web experiences.

```
<meta name="viewport" content="width=device-width">
```

To quote Peter-Paul Koch, who has written about viewports and mobile development extensively (http://bkaprt.com/mf/56):

Normally the layout viewport takes a width that the vendor has decided is optimal for viewing desktop sites. By setting the meta viewport to device-width you're sure that your site's width is optimized for the device it's being viewed on.

Viewports can also help manage differences in pixel density. Pixel density (or ppi) measures the resolution of a screen by looking at the total number of pixels available horizontally and vertically within specific physical dimensions. Apple's original iPhone had 320×480 pixels available on a 3.5in screen, which meant it had a pixel density of 164ppi. The Google Nexus One had 480×800 pixels available on a 3.7in screen, which meant it had 252ppi. Why does this make a difference?

Pixel density impacts how physically big or small elements appear on a screen. A higher pixel density means each pixel is physically smaller. Consider a set of buttons viewed on an Apple Cinema Display, which has a ppi common to many desktop computers of about 94ppi. View the same pixels on a Nokia N900, which has a pixel density of 266ppi, and you can clearly see the difference. What was large and legible is now tiny and invisible (**FIG 7.1**).

When you design for devices with different pixel densities, these differences can become a problem. On the web, however, the viewport width that mobile browsers use can help us manage this issue. As Peter-Paul Koch pointed out (http://bkaprt.com/mf/56), Apple's first set of iPhones (164ppi), Google's Nexus One (252ppi), and the iPhone 4 (329ppi) all used the same device-width of 320 pixels.

This provides some much needed layout consistency across the various pixel density devices out there. Where we still need to do some work, though, is with high-resolution images. Unlike browser-rendered controls, text, and visual elements, image files won't automatically adjust to higher pixel density screens. They'll render at the correct size but lack crispness and definition when pixel density is high (**FIG 7.2**).

To account for this, you'll need two sets of images: one large (twice the resolution) and one at standard resolution. You can then tell web browsers (using CSS3 media queries, JavaScript, or a serverside script) to only include the higher

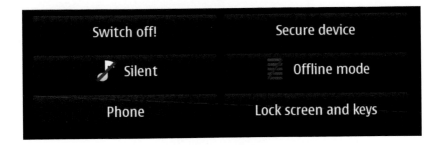

FIG 7.1: A big difference in pixels per inch (ppi) can adjust the visual size of images dramatically. Above, Apple Cinema Display (94ppi); below Nokia N900 (266ppi).

FIG 7.2: When ppi is doubled, the edges of Yahoo!'s logo image appear jagged and blurry.

resolution graphics on devices with a high-resolution display (http://bkaprt.com/mf/57).

If you're not interested in maintaining two sets of images (and who would be?), lean more heavily on CSS for your mobile web experience's visual design. The gradients and rounded corners in Yahoo!'s design (FIG 7.2) are rendered using CSS3 and look great on both high and low resolution screens, saving you the need to manage multiple images and your customers the need to download them.

Mobile browsers that don't support CSS3 properties like gradient and rounded corners can simply default to a solid background and square corners. No harm done.

Be aware though that too many CSS3 effects could diminish performance, as excessive shadows and gradients can slow down rendering on some devices. This is being addressed with faster rendering engines so it probably won't be much of an issue soon. But you've been warned nonetheless!

FLUIDLY, FLEXIBLY RESPONSIVE

Despite the fact that some mobile devices with different pixel densities will use common viewport widths, we can't count on a single width for our mobile web experiences. For starters, even if every mobile device used 320 pixels for its device-width, we'd still have different widths when one of these devices changed its orientation.

To cope with this and whatever new device widths may come our way, we need to be highly elastic in our layouts. Whether you call them fluid, liquid, or flexible, designs that expand and contract based on available screen space are a must. In a fluid layout, interface elements (like the search box and menu items in the Google Places, FIG 7.3) are designed to adapt to the space available to them.

While fluid layouts are essential, they're really just the start.

RESPONSIVE DESIGN

When the differences between screen sizes grow, flexible layouts can be stretched to their limits. Consider the layout

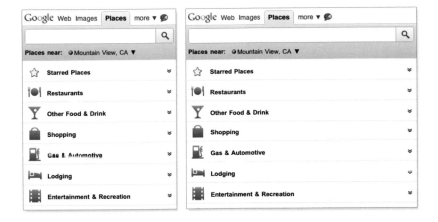

FIG 7.3: The Google Places mobile web experience uses a fluid layout to adapt to various screen widths.

possibilities on a 768 pixel device-width versus a 320 pixel device-width. Surely we can do more than just stretch the interface to fit? After all, a 768px device-width has two-and-a-half times more space! Enter responsive web design.

Through the application of fluid layouts, flexible media, CSS3 media queries, and (sometimes) a bit of JavaScript, responsive web design allows you to adapt to devices more significantly. With responsive web design, you can set a baseline (mobile) experience first, then progressively enhance or adapt your layout as device capabilities change.

This is accomplished by setting resolution "break points" and applying a different set of layout rules and media assets to each. A break point can be thought of as a conditional statement that determines if a device meets specific criteria like a minimum width of 600 pixels. If that condition is true, then the browser applies a different set of layout rules, usually through CSS, though sometimes with a little JavaScript as well. (You can get all the details in Ethan Marcotte's awesome book on the subject: http://bkaprt.com/rwd.)

These layout rules can include repositioning elements, increasing image sizes, or removing elements altogether. They

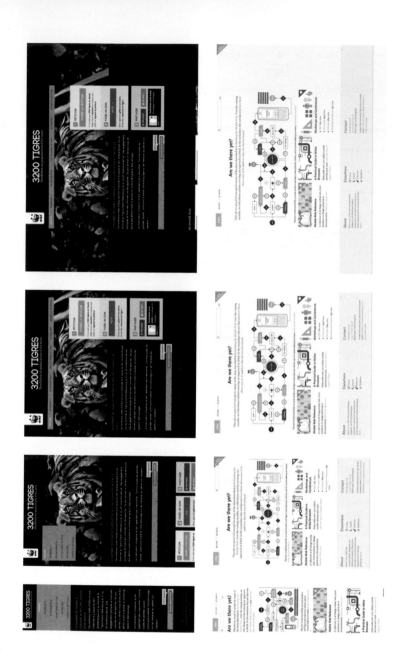

FIG 7.4: Responsive web design in action on the 3200 Tigres and Yiibu sites.

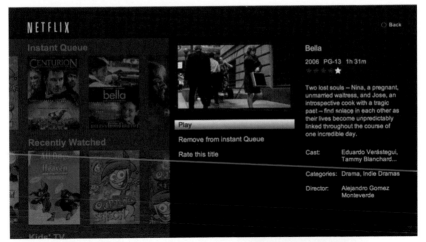

FIG 7.5: Though the Netflix experiences on the Playstation3, iPhone, and iPad are built using the same web technologies, the user interface is designed for each unique device experience.

don't have to be dramatic, but they don't have to be subtle either (**FIG 7.4**). As a different resolution break point is passed, the layout adapts to make the best use of the space available to it.

So a single web page can adapt to a large variety of screen sizes using responsive web design. But screen size isn't the only difference between devices.

DEVICE EXPERIENCES

Devices are different not just because they have different technical capabilities and limitations, but because people use them differently as well. Consider the differences between connected TVs, desktops/laptops, tablets, smartphones, and feature phones. Each of these device experiences has a unique:

- *Common user posture:* 10 foot lean-back experience on the couch, long periods of use at a desk, casual couch or bed use, or quick bursts of activity in various locations throughout the day.
- *Primary input method:* remote/gestures, mouse/keyboard, touch/sensors, keypads.
- *Average display size:* wall-sized, desk-sized, lap-sized, palm-sized, or smaller still.

The combination of these differences is often significant enough to "define" a device experience. And different device experiences may require different user interface design solutions. The relative importance of primary tasks can differ between device experiences (because of user posture), as can the layout and interaction design needed to accommodate different input modes and average display sizes.

As a result, many web applications take the time to design and develop unique solutions for distinct device experiences. For example, the movie streaming service Netflix has distinct HTML5 solutions for connected TVs, tablets, desktop web browsers, and mobile devices (**FIG 7.5**). While this requires them to maintain a number of different interfaces, each of these interfaces is optimized for the user posture, input method, and average display size of a distinct device class.

While it's possible to have a single user interface work across more than one device experience, developing a single interface that works across all device experiences may result in compromises or bare-bones features that don't take advantage of what makes each device experience excel (or, conversely, in rich solutions that fail to work on lower-end devices).

So while a connected TV could browse a text list optimized for feature phones, it is unlikely anyone would want to use it that way. On the other hand, a tablet-optimized web application might feel simpler to use on a desktop web browser because the number of actions has been reduced to work on a smaller display size, and the size of the actions has been increased to accommodate touch interactions. While this interface wouldn't be optimized for a desktop computer's user posture, input methods, or display sizes, it would still be really functional.

Device experiences can also be useful for thinking through how each break point in a responsive web design solution should not only look but act as well. Layout and media assets can be adjusted to make the best use of available screen space and to optimize for specific input capabilities (such as appropriately sized touch targets).

The right combination of device experience-specific designs, responsive web design, and fluid interfaces can ensure your mobile web experiences work on today's mobile devices and beyond.

But there's still one more thing.

REDUCE

Just in case it hasn't been made abundantly clear in this book, I want to remind you that reduction is the best layout approach available to you on mobile. Appropriately sized touch targets need room to respond to our imprecise fingers. Responsive web designs need to adapt to a variety of screen sizes and resolutions. Distinct device experience solutions need to be maintained as content and features change and grow.

All of these factors push us toward less on our screens—fewer variations to manage and fewer options for people to consider and select without making errors. Across all your mobile layouts, aim for the minimum amount necessary to help people meet their needs whether they're looking up or finding information, exploring and playing, checking in on important updates, or editing and creating content.

Not only will reduction make putting mobile layouts together easier, it will also give people focused ways to get things done. If you start to hear customers asking for your desktop web experience to be more like the simple, easy-to-use mobile one—you're doing it right.

LAYING OUT THE LAND

As the mobile landscape continues to change, we have to be ready with layouts that adapt to the task at hand—from big differences between device experiences to filling in the small gaps between device screen sizes and orientations.

- Accept and embrace the rate of change in mobile isn't going to change anytime soon.
- Use the meta viewport tag to let mobile browsers know you've thought of them in your designs.
- Account for differences in screen density by making higher resolution images available to the devices that support them.
- Adapt to device variations with responsive and fluid layouts.
- Account for the differences between device experiences in your responsive web design or server-side solutions.
- Reduce complexity for yourself and your customers by cutting down to the minimum amount of functionality necessary for your website or application.

Though we've covered a number of techniques for managing our layouts across an ever-increasing number of devices, there's more to come. As mobile continues to grow and the definition of what a "mobile" device is continues to blur, expect new techniques for managing layout to emerge. In other words, watch this space.

CONCLUSION

At this point, I hope the small idea of designing and building for mobile first has given you lots of big ideas for the web. Today's mobile device is our true personal computer: always with us, connected to the network, and filled with new capabilities for getting things done, communicating with each other, and just killing some time. Starting with this personal and portable device in mind first allows us to:

- Take advantage of the enormous growth in mobile internet usage and find new ways for people to use our websites and applications.
- Embrace mobile constraints to focus and prioritize the services we're designing and building.
- Use mobile capabilities to innovate the complete customer experience.
- Take what we know about designing for the web and start thinking differently about mobile organization, actions, inputs, and layout.

It doesn't take a lot more than that but here's a few parting tips to help you along.

- Whenever possible, test your designs and code on actual mobile devices. Simulators and desktop browsers are not substitutes for the real thing.
- If you can't get your hands on a few mobile devices, head over to a local mobile device shop and look at your mobile web experience on their floor models.
- Prototype, prototype, prototype. The sooner a mobile web experience is in your hands, the faster you'll know if it works in the real world.

And last but not least, don't be afraid to start small. Some of the biggest successes in mobile today came from small experiments and teams of passionate web designers and developers. You don't need to know everything about mobile—just take what you do know and *go.*

BIG THANKS

Writing a book, no matter how small, is a big undertaking. Thankfully I got a lot of help along the way. Jeffrey Zeldman, Eric Meyer, and the entire An Event Apart crew gave me the chance to talk Mobile First for the first time at their wonderful web conference. There, and everywhere else I presented my Mobile First ideas, I received invaluable feedback and questions that helped shape and refine what's in this book.

Extra detailed feedback and many big ideas came from my esteemed set of technical reviewers: Bryan and Stephanie Rieger, Jason Grigsby, Craig Villamor, Peter Paul Koch, Josh Clark, and a little bit of Ethan Marcotte (that went a long way). Listening is just as vital to creating a book as writing, and these were the people I spent a lot of time listening to over the past few years.

When it came time to actually turn ideas into words, the A Book Apart team made it easy. My editor Mandy Brown, copyeditor Krista Stevens, designer extraordinaire Jason Santa Maria, and ringmaster Jeffrey Zeldman were an absolute joy to work with.

None of this, though, would be possible without the endless support of my wife Amanda. With our new baby girl, two-year old son, my start-up, and my non-stop travel schedule, she somehow believed I was not totally out of my mind when I decided to write a book as well. Perhaps she was the only one, which is why this book is lovingly dedicated to her.

RESOURCES

More data, please

Morgan Stanley's Mobile Internet Report was a huge source of supporting facts and information for me. It's filled with hundreds of slides with data about the biggest trends in mobile (http://bkaprt.com/mf/58).

Mary Meeker was the primary author of the Mobile Internet Report and has gone on to publish more of her findings in her new role at Kleiner Perkins (http://bkaprt.com/mf/59).

For ongoing mobile market information and data, keep up with Horace Dediu's articles and pointers on Asymco (http://bkaprt.com/mf/60).

I also publish design-related data points about mobile computing and more every Monday on my blog (http://bkaprt.com/mf/61).

Mobile first development

While this book doesn't dig into mobile first web development, others have.

Bryan and Stephanie Rieger's write-up about the construction of their site, Yiibu, outlines how they approached markup, style sheets, and content development (http://bkaprt.com/mf/62).

Ethan Marcotte's *Responsive Web Design* book outlines how flexible grids, flexible images, and media queries can be used to adapt web site layouts across many devices (http://bkaprt.com/rwd).

The Cloud Four blog is filled with many great articles about the intersection of mobile devices and the web (http://bkaprt.com/mf/63).

The great debates

Everything in technology and design gets debated and mobile is no different. Here are a few summaries of some of the thornier issues still being discussed.

Native mobile applications vs. mobile web solutions: when does each one make sense and why (http://bkaprt.com/mf/64, http://bkaprt.com/mf/65)?

Can we really understand and design for mobile context? Jason Grigsby sums up the issues and provides links to many pertinent articles (http://bkaprt.com/mf/66).

And last but not least: separate mobile web pages or responsive web design? It depends, says Josh Clark in his summary of the issue (http://bkaprt.com/mf/67).

REFERENCES

Shortened URLs are numbered sequentially; the related long URLs are listed below for reference.

Introduction

1 http://www.lukew.com/ff/entry.asp?1270
2 http://www.lukew.com/ff/entry.asp?1226
3 http://www.lukew.com/ff/entry.asp?1225

Chapter 1

4 http://www.smartonline.com/smarton-products/smarton-mobile/
smartphones-pass-pc-sales-for-the-first-time-in-history/

5 http://articles.businessinsider.com/2011-02-15/tech/29983706_1_tablet-
market-pcs-smartphones

6 http://www.comscore.com/Press_Events/Press_Releases/2011/1/Web-
based_Email_Shows_Signs_of_Decline_in_the_U.S._While_Mobile_Email_
Usage_on_the_Rise

7 http://news.bango.com/2010/02/16/600-percent-growth-in-mobile-web-
usage/

8 http://mobithinking.com/mobile-marketing-tools/latest-mobile-stats

9 http://www.morganstanley.com/institutional/techresearch/pdfs/MS_
Economy_Internet_Trends_102009_FINAL.pdf

10 http://www.mediapost.com/publications/?fa=Articles.showArticle&art_
aid=120590

11 http://www.lukew.com/ff/entry.asp?1361

12 http://www.lukew.com/ff/entry.asp?1269

13 http://techcrunch.com/2010/12/13/google-mobile-searches-grew-130-
percent-in-q3/

14 http://www.mobiadnews.com/?p=5133

15 http://www.youtube.com/watch?v=8aaOtVJQcg0

16 http://en.wikipedia.org/wiki/T9_(predictive_text)

17 http://www.cisco.com/en/US/solutions/collateral/ns341/ns525/ns537/
ns705/ns827/white_paper_c11-520862.html

18 http://www.comscore.com/Press_Events/Press_Releases/2010/3/
Facebook_and_Twitter_Access_via_Mobile_Browser_Grows_by_Triple-
Digits

19 http://newsroom.cisco.com/dlls/ekits/Cisco_VNI_Global_Mobile_Data_
    Traffic_Forecast_2010_2015.pdf

20 http://www.gartner.com/it/page.jsp?id=1466313

21 http://blog.admob.com/2008/12/18/impact-of-new-rim-handsets-storm-
    rising/

22 http://officialblog.yelp.com/2011/02/via-yelp-mobile-yelpers-call-a-local-
    business-every-other-second.html

23 http://www.lukew.com/ff/entry.asp?1131

24 http://www.cloudfour.com/links-do-not-open-apps

25 http://blog.twitter.com/2010/09/evolving-ecosystem.html

26 http://danzarrella.com/new-data-on-mobile-facebook-posting.html

27 http://www.facebook.com/press/info.php?statistics

28 http://joehewitt.com/post/ipad/

Chapter 2

29 https://developer.mozilla.org/en/canvas_tutorial

30 http://www.html5rocks.com/en/tutorials/appcache/beginner/

31 http://googleresearch.blogspot.com/2009/06/speed-matters.html

32 http://blog.compete.com/2010/03/12/smartphone-owners-a-ready-and-
    willing-audience/

33 http://readitlaterlist.com/blog/2011/01/is-mobile-affecting-when-we-read/

34 http://www.lukew.com/ff/entry.asp?1259

Chapter 3

35 http://itunes.apple.com/us/app/nearest-tube/id322436683?mt=8

36 http://stackoverflow.com/questions/1649086/detect-rotation-of-android-
    phone-in-the-browser-with-javascript

37 http://mail.glustech.com/SnowGlobe/

38 http://thenextweb.com/apps/2010/12/21/hidden-safari-mobile-feature-
    reveals-augmented-reality-capability/

Chapter 4

39 http://www.dmolsen.com/mobile-in-higher-ed/2011/02/07/the-university-
    home-page-mobile-first/

40 http://xkcd.com/773/

Chapter 5

41 http://paidcontent.org/article/419-pontiflex-about-half-of-mobile-app-clicks-are-accidental/

42 http://developer.apple.com/library/ios/#documentation/UserExperience/Conceptual/MobileHIG/Introduction/Introduction.html

43 http://www.lukew.com/ff/entry.asp?1085

44 http://go.microsoft.com/?linkid=9713252

45 http://www.lukew.com/touch

46 http://www.lukew.com/ff/entry.asp?1197

47 http://en.wikipedia.org/wiki/Progressive_enhancement

Chapter 6

48 http://www.lukew.com/ff/entry.asp?1198

49 http://mashable.com/2010/08/07/ebay-facts/

50 http://mashable.com/2011/01/07/40-of-all-tweets-come-from-mobile/

51 http://www.lukew.com/ff/entry.asp?691

52 http://www.medien.ifi.lmu.de/pubdb/publications/pub/deluca2007pmc/deluca2007pmc.pdf

53 http://www.lukew.com/ff/entry.asp?1235

54 http://diveintohtml5.org/

55 http://www.quirksmode.org/html5/inputs_mobile.html

Chapter 7

56 http://www.quirksmode.org/blog/archives/2010/09/combining_meta.html

57 http://www.lukew.com/ff/entry.asp?1142

Resources

58 http://www.morganstanley.com/institutional/techresearch/mobile_internet_report122009.html

59 http://www.slideshare.net/kleinerperkins/kpcb-top-10-mobile-trends-feb-2011

60 http://www.asymco.com/

61 http://lukew.com/ff

62 http://yiibu.com/about/site/index.html

63 http://www.cloudfour.com/category/mobile-web-and-services/

64 http://www.lukew.com/ff/entry.asp?1337
65 http://www.lukew.com/ff/entry.asp?1193
66 http://www.cloudfour.com/on-mobile-context/
67 http://globalmoxie.com/blog/mobile-web-responsive-design.shtml

INDEX

ABOUT A BOOK APART

Web design is about multi-disciplinary mastery and laser focus, and that's the thinking behind our brief books for people who make websites. We cover the emerging and essential topics in web design and development with style, clarity, and, above all, brevity—because working designer-developers can't afford to waste time.

The goal of every title in our catalog is to shed clear light on a tricky subject, and do it fast, so you can get back to work. Thank you for supporting our mission to provide professionals with the tools they need to move the web forward.

COLOPHON

The text is set in FF Yoga and its companion, FF Yoga Sans, both by Xavier Dupré. Headlines and cover are set in Titling Gothic by David Berlow, code excerpts in Consolas by Lucas de Groot.

ABOUT THE AUTHOR

 Luke was Co-founder and Chief Product Officer (CPO) of Bagcheck (http://bagcheck.com/) which was acquired by Twitter, Inc., just nine months after being launched publicly. Prior to this, Luke was an Entrepreneur in Residence (EIR) at Benchmark Capital and the Chief Design Architect (VP) at Yahoo! Inc. where he worked on product alignment and forward-thinking integrated customer experiences on the web, mobile, TV, and beyond.

Luke is the author of two popular web design books—*Web Form Design* (Rosenfeld Media, 2008) and *Site-Seeing: A Visual Approach to Web Usability* (Wiley, 2002)—and many articles about digital product design and strategy. He is also a top-rated speaker at conferences and companies around the world, and a Co-founder and former Board member of the Interaction Design Association (IxDA).

Previously, Luke was the Lead User Interface Designer of eBay Inc.'s platform team, where he led the strategic design of new consumer products (such as eBay Express and Kijiji) and internal tools and processes. He also founded LukeW Ideation & Design (http://www.lukew.com/), a product strategy and design consultancy; taught graduate interface design courses at the University of Illinois; and worked as a Senior Interface Designer at the National Center for Supercomputing Applications (NCSA), the birthplace of the first popular graphical web browser, NCSA Mosaic.